WINNING OTHERS TO CHRIST

A Study for Personal Workers

by

W. E. REED

THE GOSPEL TRUMPET COMPANY
Publication Board of the Church of God
Anderson, Indiana

Printed in the United States of America

PREFACE

The title of this book expresses its purpose—that of helping others find Christ. Emphasis is placed directly on the need, message, motives, and methods of evangelism. When the need is recognized and the motive for evangelism is supplied by a vital experience of Christ in the soul, methods will invariably be found to take the Christian witness to others. Once found, the methods will be adjusted to fit any given situation in which the individual Christian finds himself. As the Apostle Paul expressed it: "I am made all things to all men, that I might by all means save some." The evangelistic heart will find its method.

The writer humbly wishes to acknowledge his indebtedness to the many writers on evangelism from whose works he has received insights into the Christian's task and responsibility. An honest attempt has been made to give recognition to other writers when their materials have been consciously used.

Many helpful books have been written on evangelism, yet the subject is inexhaustible. It is hoped that this book will serve a useful purpose in stimulating Christians to help others find Christ.

February 1953

> W. E. REED
> Secretary of Evangelism
> Board of Church Extension
>   and Home Missions
> Church of God, Anderson, Ind.

OTHERS

Brightly beams our Savior's message,
Which was sent from shore to shore:
It was simply one word—"Others"
And 'twill live for evermore.

Bear ye one another's burdens:
This the law of Christ doth say;
And, like Him, preferring others,
In that self-forgetful way.

If you live your life for others,
You, yourself, shall blessed be;
When to others you take blessings,
Blessings will return to thee.

Let me live my life for others;
Others, let my motto be;
Help me, Lord, to do for others
As I would they'd do for me.

(Tune: "Let the Lower Lights Be Burning")

CONTENTS

Chapter		Page
I.	Jesus Christ Came to Save	7
II.	Why Win Others to Christ?	23
III.	How Jesus Won Others	41
IV.	Ways of Winning Others	59
V.	More Ways of Winning Others	83

Winning Others to Christ

CHAPTER I

JESUS CHRIST CAME TO SAVE

Concerning the purpose of his coming into the world, Jesus said: "The Son of man is come to seek and to save that which was lost" (Luke 19:10). And again: "The Son of man came not to be ministered unto, but to minister, and to give his life a ransom for many" (Matt. 20:28). Paul further attested this purpose by writing: "This is a faithful saying, and worthy of all acceptation, that Christ Jesus came into the world to save sinners" (I Tim. 1:15). Christians in every age have found in this purpose of Christ a tremendous motive for evangelism.

> *We have heard the joyful sound:*
> *Jesus saves! Jesus saves!*
> *Spread the tidings all around:*
> *Jesus saves! Jesus saves!*
> *Bear the news to every land,*
> *Climb the steeps and cross the waves;*
> *Onward! 'Tis our Lord's command:*
> *Jesus saves! Jesus saves!*
> —Priscilla J. Owens

How does Christ save? From what does Christ save? For what does Christ save? What are the conditions for salvation? These are all questions which the person who seeks to help others find Christ must be prepared to answer.

7

How Does Jesus Christ Save?

The New Testament presents four answers to this question:

1. Christ saves by the example of his holy life.
2. Christ saves by the accomplishment of his death.
3. Christ saves by the power of his resurrection.
4. Christ saves by the effectiveness of his mediation.

Let us consider each answer in its order.

Jesus Christ Saves by His Life

Christ saves by the example of his holy life. The life of Jesus exhibits the divine ideal of man. We understand what is meant by our creation in the image of God when we behold Jesus. In him we are able to see what God desires to see in every man. By his life, subjected as he was to all the temptations common to man, yet without sin, he revealed the highest possibilities of life in this world. The example of his life speaks to our lives at all points of moral living. Of him it is written: "Christ also suffered for us, leaving us an example, that we should follow his steps: who did no sin, neither was guile found in his mouth" (I Pet. 2:21-22).

In speech, Jesus was blameless. Truth found perfect expression in him. Those who heard him said: "Never man spake like this man." He spoke with moral and spiritual authority. Of his own words, he said: "The words that I speak unto you, they are spirit, and they are life" (John 6:63). He warned that "every idle word that men shall speak, they shall give account thereof in the day of judgment" (Matt. 12:36). When one considers that more sin is committed by word of mouth than in any other way, the example of Christ is more deeply appreciated. "When he was reviled, he reviled not again."

In spirit, Jesus was magnanimous. The criterion of

Christian experience is the presence of Christ's Spirit in one's life. "If any man have not the Spirit of Christ, he is none of his. . . . For as many as are led by the Spirit of God, they are the sons of God" (Rom. 8:9, 14). When James and John asked if He would have them call down fire from heaven and destroy certain Samaritans, he said to them: "Ye know not what manner of spirit ye are of. For the Son of man is not come to destroy men's lives, but to save them" (Luke 9:55-56). In his presence men became conscious of their sins.

In service, Jesus was sublime. He related everything he did to the will of God, testifying: "My meat is to do the will of him that sent me, and to finish his work" (John 4:34). As he closed his earthly ministry, he reminded his Father in prayer: "I have finished the work which thou gavest me to do." In all things he pleased God. No other person has ever lived so selflessly. He utterly abandoned himself to doing the will of God and to bringing salvation to man. The manner of his life and service is a standard for our lives. Paul exalts his example and exhorts: "Let this mind be in you, which was also in Christ Jesus: who, being in the form of God, thought it not robbery to be equal with God: but made himself of no reputation, and took upon him the form of a servant, and was made in the likeness of men: and being found in fashion as a man, he humbled himself, and became obedient unto death, even the death of the cross" (Phil. 2:5-8).

Following the example of Jesus consists of far more than patterning our lives after his. In fact, before this can really be done the corrupted moral nature of man must be transformed and renewed.

Jesus Christ Saves by His Death

Jesus Christ saves by the accomplishments of his atoning death. The purpose of Jesus' life was death.

This is a strange paradox; nevertheless it is true. Jesus came to put a finish to the dominion of sin; in order to do this, he had to die. But death to Jesus was not the cutting short of his career; it was the supreme purpose in his life. Of his own death, he said: "I lay down my life, that I might take it again. No man taketh it from me, but I lay it down of myself. I have power to lay it down, and I have power to take it again. This commandment have I received of my Father" (John 10:17-18). When Jesus was transfigured on the mountain, Moses and Elijah appeared from the glory world and "spake with him of his decease which he should accomplish at Jerusalem" (Luke 9:31). That word *accomplish* deserves to be underscored, for it is the key to his passion and death.

What did the death of Jesus accomplish? Seven hundred years before Jesus died the prophet Isaiah foresaw these accomplishments of his death: "He was wounded for our transgressions, he was bruised for our iniquities: the chastisement of our peace was upon him; and with his stripes we are healed" (Isa. 53:5). God's plan of salvation is complete, covering the total needs of the total man—forgiveness for our volitional sins, cleansing from our sinful natures, peace for our distressed minds, and healing for our diseased and afflicted bodies. No area of man's life is omitted.

The writers of the New Testament use several different words to describe the accomplishments of Jesus' death: redemption, remission, reconciliation, regeneration, justification, propitiation, and forgiveness. Though there is a difference in the meaning of these terms, what they describe is all included in the same experience of grace in the soul, and it all takes place at one and the same time. Jesus' death secures for us the adoption of sons into God's family (Gal. 4:5), preservation from wickedness (1:4), freedom from iniquity (Titus 2:14), reconciliation with God (II Cor. 5:19), and the promise of the Spirit of God (Rom. 8:15). It assures us that Christ is Lord both of the dead and the living (14:9).

Jesus Christ Saves by His Resurrection

Jesus Christ saves by the justifying power of his resurrection. The resurrection of Christ from the dead demonstrates his victory over sin and declares God's acceptance of the atonement he made. This act of God, more than any other, guarantees the validity of the Christian gospel. "If Christ be not raised, your faith is vain; ye are yet in your sins" (I Cor. 15:17). The gospel is predicated upon the promise that God will not impute sin against us if "we believe on him that raised up Jesus our Lord from the dead; who was delivered for our offenses, and was raised again for our justification" (Rom. 4:24-25). Gospel justification is that act of God's free grace by which sinful man, when he repents toward God and has faith in the atonement and resurrection of Christ, is acquitted of all past wrongs and looked upon by God as if he had never committed sin.

As a summation of the accomplishments of Christ's life, death, and resurrection, the Apostle Paul writes: "But God commendeth his love toward us, in that, while we were yet sinners, Christ died for us. Much more then, being now justified by his blood, we shall be saved from wrath through him. For if, when we were enemies, we were reconciled to God by the death of his Son, much more, being reconciled, we shall be saved by his life."

Jesus Christ Saves by His Mediation

Jesus Christ saves by the effectiveness of his mediation. The work of Christ for our salvation did not end when he ascended to heaven. He completed the work of redemption in order to assume the work of mediation. "God . . . will have all men to be saved, and to come unto the knowledge of the truth. For there is one God, and one mediator between God and men, the man Christ Jesus, who gave himself a ransom for all" (I Tim. 2:3-6). The writer to the Hebrews further describes the continuing work of Christ as that of a great High Priest who "is able to save them to the uttermost that come unto God by him, seeing he ever liveth to make intercession for them" (7:25).

FROM WHAT DOES JESUS CHRIST SAVE?

Christ saves from selfishness, from sin, and from religious sectarianism. He saves fully and completely. The angel announced concerning him: "Thou shalt call his name Jesus: for he shall save his people from their sins" (Matt. 1:21).

Jesus Christ Saves from Selfishness

The tree of sin has a great number of branches and bears a variety of fruits, but it has only one taproot— the root of inordinate selfishness. Jesus traced all the moral evil of the world to the tendency of men to care for themselves too much and for others too little. Over against this tendency towards self-love he placed two commandments of love: "Thou shalt love the Lord thy God with all thy heart, and with all thy soul, and with all thy mind. . . . Thou shalt love thy neighbor as thyself" (Matt. 22:37, 39). Jesus aimed at the complete subordination of self-love to love for God and man. The self-love he condemned was that which took nothing and nobody into its calculations but self.

All the sins of individuals and of society have developed from inordinate and excessive self-love. Jesus attacked this evil in the heart of man with mockery and denouncement. He described a certain rich man as saying: "What shall *I* do, because *I* have no room where to bestow *my* fruits? And he said, This will *I* do: *I* will pull down *my* barns, and build greater; and there will *I* bestow all *my* fruits and *my* goods. And *I* will say to *my* soul, Soul, thou hast much goods laid up for many years; take *thine* ease, eat, drink, and be merry" (Luke 12:17-19).

Such self-absorption was repugnant to Jesus, and he quotes God as saying: "Thou fool." He insisted that life is attained only by forgetting oneself. "Whosoever shall seek to save his life shall lose it; and whosoever shall lose his life shall preserve it" (Luke 17:33). He made self-denial the first condition for discipleship: "If any man will come after me, let him deny himself." To deny oneself, according to Jesus, is to recognize, acknowledge, and accept the claims of God and of one's fellows, to subordinate self-interest to love for God and man. This is the central idea of morality and ethics revealed by Jesus.

Jesus Christ Saves from Sin

Two kinds of sin attracted the attention of Jesus—the sins of the flesh and the sins of the spirit, the sins of action and the sins of attitude. Concerning the sins of the flesh, Jesus had but little to say. This does not mean that he treated this kind of sin with lightness or indifference, but that he traced sin to its lair in the heart. When he spoke against the sin of adultery he laid the ax at the source of the sin. "Whosoever looketh on a woman to lust after her hath committed adultery with her already in his heart" (Matt. 5:28). Jesus recognized that the sins of the flesh cannot be cured by fierce denunciation of them, but rather by an inward change of ideals and purposes.

The sins of the spirit came in for his strongest condemnation. Pride, self-will, self-righteousness, resentment, self-sufficiency, blindness to one's own faults, hypocrisy, and even negative goodness received his denunciation both directly and in parables. He found the fountainhead of sin in the heart of man: "For from within, out of the heart of man, proceed evil thoughts, adulteries, fornications, murders, thefts, covetousness, wickedness, deceit, lasciviousness, an evil eye, blasphemy, pride, foolishness: all these evil things come from within, and defile the man" (Mark 7:21-23).

Jesus dealt drastically and severely with sin. He condemned it wherever it appeared. In his life he gave it no place, by his death he won freedom from it for those who trust in him, and by his resurrection he makes possible the regeneration of man from its corruption and defilement. "For this purpose the Son of God was manifested, that he might destroy the works of the devil" (I John 3:8). Jesus Christ reaches to the "uttermost" part of human nature and perfects regeneration and cleansing. Jesus Christ saves from sin, all kinds of sin. Not only does he save from sin, he keeps the soul from sinning. He saves his people *from* (out of, forth from) their sins.

Jesus Christ Saves from Sectarianism

Religion is not always a good thing; sometimes it is bad, very bad. Jesus found among his contemporaries much bad religion and condemned it without mercy. Most of his opposition came from those who paraded themselves as being the chosen people of God. He observed that some who professed religion were loveless and pitiless in their treatment of their fellow men, harsh in their judgments, unwilling to forgive, oppressive, and morally blind. He attacked religious bigotry, hypocrisy, and false piety with pronouncements of woe. He accused certain representatives of religion of shutting "up the kingdom of heaven against men: for ye neither go in yourselves, neither suffer ye them that are entering to go in." He further indicted them: "Ye compass sea and land to make one proselyte, and when he is made, ye make him twofold more the child of hell than yourselves" (Matt. 23:15).

What would Jesus say about sectarianism and religious bigotry if he lived in our world today? Would he condemn the multiplicity of divisions and denominations that are actually competing with each other to make disciples unto him? Would he condemn the substitution of churchianity for Christianity, church membership for conversion? These are questions that will not down. Those who would help others find Christ must face them and answer them in the spirit of Christ. In the truest sense, there is no difference between being a Christian and being a member of the church which is the body of Christ. "For by one spirit are we all baptized into one body, whether we be Jews or Gentiles, whether we be bond or free; and have been all made to drink into one Spirit" (I Cor. 12:13). Those who go to make disciples for Christ need to remember that the ultimate goal of their mission is conversion and not merely church membership.

Jesus prescribed a cure for sectarianism for all who will receive it. He said to his disciples: "If ye continue in my word, then are ye my disciples indeed; and ye shall know the truth, and the truth shall make you free" (John 8:31-32). Men tend to become sectarian at the point of crystallizing their viewpoints regarding truth without recognizing its universality and the possibility that they are seeing only a segment of truth. Those who follow Christ need to recognize that truth is always progressive in its revelation and that there is always more to it than is immediately seen. The Spirit of Christ is the Spirit of truth. "When he, the Spirit of truth, is come, he will guide you into all truth." No man can follow the Spirit of Christ and remain sectarian in either his attitude or practice.

For What Does Jesus Christ Save?

What objective did God have in mind when he provided a plan of redemption for man? What is the purpose of man's salvation? What does Christ expect to accomplish through saving man from sin?

Jesus Christ Saves Us to Live with Him

In explaining the purpose of salvation, Paul writes: "For God hath not appointed us to wrath, but to obtain salvation by our Lord Jesus Christ, who died for us, that, whether we wake or sleep, we should live together with him" (I Thess. 5:9-10). These closing words express the purpose of our salvation clearly and distinctly: "That . . . we should live together with him."

To be a Christian is a matter of personal relationship with Christ. It is a relation rooted in heart trust rather than in head knowledge. There is a difference between knowing a person and knowing about a person. Quite a file of information can be developed about a person— date and place of birth, names of parents, color of hair and eyes—without knowing the person. Not many people in America today are entirely ignorant of Jesus. They know he was born in Bethlehem, grew up in Nazareth, at thirty years began to teach and heal, after three years was crucified and rose from the dead. No other person is so widely known about as Jesus; yet amazingly few people know him. Paul's statement concerning what it means to be a Jew could well be paraphrased to express what it means to be a Christian: "For he is not a Christian who is one outwardly." But he is a Christian who is one inwardly, for Christianity is of the heart, in the spirit, and not in the letter." (See Romans 2:28-29.)

Since being a Christian is a personal relationship, rooted in heart trust, it must be renewed continually. This is true of all personal relationships. A man and woman marry in order to live together. Marriage is a relationship that demands renewal. The wife cannot live on the affection of ten years ago, five years ago, last month. So it is with the Christian's relationship with Christ. It is not enough to have been converted and baptized years ago. The only thing that counts in the Christian life is daily living "together with Christ." If our relationship with Christ is to remain warm and vital, we must daily keep in touch with him. By speaking to him constantly in prayer and by diligently reading his Word, we perpetually renew and strengthen our relation with Christ.

Jesus Christ Saves Us to Work with Him

The task of the Christian is to help others find Christ. That task defines evangelism in its simplest terms, yet it expresses its most comprehensive meaning. It requires, first of all, that Christ shall be so fully and intelligently known that it becomes natural to make him known to others. When a person finds Christ for himself and is soundly converted, the saving process is only started.

It is under the inspiration of love and devotion to Christ that men become untiring servants and faithful stewards of the gospel message. Once Christ is truly experienced, nothing really matters except the finding of the work he would have one do and then doing it with full dedication of life. As Paul expressed it: "One died for all . . . that they which live should not henceforth live unto themselves, but unto him which died for them, and rose again" (II Cor. 5:14-15).

Jesus Christ Saves Us to Dwell with Him

There is a *plus* in the Christian religion. On the eve of his crucifixion Jesus talked with his disciples about what they could expect if they kept their faith steadfast in him: "Let not your heart be troubled: ye believe in God, believe also in me. In my Father's house are many mansions: if it were not so, I would have told you. I go to prepare a place for you. And if I go and prepare a place for you, I will come again, and receive you unto myself; that where I am, there ye may be also" (John 14:1-3). These words have furnished an incentive to the disciples of Christ across the years to keep faith in the gospel and to continue their witness.

The Christian gospel underwrites life with hope. The hope which man lost through sin was restored through Christ through whom God "hath begotten us again unto a lively hope by the resurrection of Jesus Christ from the dead, to an inheritance incorruptible and undefiled, and that fadeth not away, reserved in heaven for you" (I Pet. 1:3-4). This hope serves as a restraining and compelling influence upon the followers of Christ in everything they say and do. It restrains them from returning to the former life of sin and death; it compels them to live worthy of their vocation.

How Can Man Be Saved?

"What must I do to be saved?" is a question frequently asked. The question was asked by the Philippian jailer of Paul and Silas (Acts 16:25-34). Using his conversion as a guide in our study, let us note the four steps that are plainly evident and essential to a definite experience of salvation.

Man Must Be Awakened

Of the jailer, we read: "And the keeper of the prison, awaking out of his sleep . . ." Here was the starting point of his salvation. He was awakened suddenly and dramatically by "a great earthquake." Awaking, he was gripped with pungent fear, and he started to take his own life. But the voice of Paul stopped him. Fortunate for this man that Paul and Silas were in jail on this night! They knew his need and how to help him.

God employs various means to awaken the unsaved. In this instance he used a physical calamity connected with a personal witness. Sometimes he uses the example of a holy life, a deep personal sorrow, the testimony of a faithful Christian, a gospel sermon, a piece of literature, the direct visitation of his Spirit, or any one of a thousand different ways. The important thing is the awakening. It can be rightly said that "God works in all things to awaken the lost and bring sinners to repentance." Without the awakening, there can be no conversion. It all begins with the recognition of the need. Christians by their lives, their prayers, their witnessing, their helpfulness, are of tremendous importance in bringing about this awakening. These the Spirit uses to convince the sinner of his sin and of God's demands upon him for righteousness. It is the Spirit who awakens and convicts, but he often uses the blameless life of Christians as his instruments.

Man Must Be Enlightened

To be awakened is not enough. Though awake, the jailer was yet in the dark and could not see his way. His second step towards salvation reads: "He called for a light." Having no light of his own, and sensing the urgency of his situation, he called for someone else to provide light for him. How descriptive of the sinner's condition in sin. In the Bible the sinner is described as blind, walking in darkness. Many a man has been awakened to his need of God but has not known how to find God. Again, it was fortunate for the jailer that Paul and Silas were in jail with him. But what of the non-Christians across the world who know the power of sin but who do not know how to find salvation? They grope their way in spiritual darkness, making crude attempts to appease their pagan gods.

The task of the Christian becomes clear here. Ours is the task of sharing the light of the gospel of Christ with those who know it not. We are to "shine as lights in the world, holding forth the word of life" (Phil. 2:15-16). All about us are endless numbers of boys and girls, men and women, living within easy reach of the church who are as spiritually blind and unenlightened as this poor jailer. These people need the gospel, must have the gospel, or they will be eternally lost. To what extent are we who are Christian responsible for the unsaved? What if Paul and Silas had remained silent one minute longer? Cannot our witness be used of God to awaken and enlighten some unsaved soul near us?

Man Must Be Obedient

After calling for a light, the jailer "sprang in, and came trembling, and fell down before Paul and Silas, and brought them out, and said, Sirs, what must I do to be saved?" His action indicates a complete change of attitude, with a view toward getting right with God. When he imprisoned Paul and Silas, he lacerated their backs with the Roman scourge, not thinking what a few hours would bring. Now the tables are turned. His conviction of sin is leading him to repentance. This is right and proper, for the salvation of the soul cannot be effected without repentance. "Godly sorrow worketh repentance to salvation" (II Cor. 7:10).

What is involved in repentance? Repentance is an attitude which brings man to a new realization of his relationship with God, an act by which he brings himself to a point of alignment and co-operation with God's will. More particularly, it is a reversal of one's rebellious attitude toward God and a return to a mind obediently responsive to the love and grace of God. It includes contrition and sorrow for past sins, confession of sins to God and so far as necessary and advisable, to man, and the making of whatever restitution is possible and required by God. As an open declaration of his willingness to obey the known commands of the gospel, the jailer took Paul and Silas "the same hour of the night and washed their stripes, and was baptized." His repentance found expression in both his attitude and his action.

Man Must Believe on Jesus Christ

The final step in the jailer's salvation reads: "He ... rejoiced, believing in God with all his house." That which was begun in the darkness and frustration of an awakened conscience now finds joyful fulfillment in the faith of the Christian gospel. That gospel emanates from a person, Jesus Christ. He is the gospel. The jailer did not find salvation by believing certain facts about Christ, but by believing on Christ himself. He had never heard of Christ before this night, but as the plan of salvation was unfolded by faithful witnesses, the jailer made his heart obedient to the gospel and took the step of faith toward Christ. The result: salvation. This is the inevitable result attained by all who follow a conscience awakened and enlightened by the gospel to repentance "toward God and faith toward our Lord Jesus Christ" (Acts 20:21).

What does it mean to believe on the Lord Jesus Christ? It means that those who desire to be saved must center their faith in him and in his finished work of redemption. No man can make an adequate atonement for his own sins; therefore, if he is to be saved, he must look beyond himself and through the atonement made by Christ find his way to salvation. "By grace are ye saved through faith; and that not of yourselves: it is the gift of God: not of works, lest any man should boast" (Eph. 2: 8-9). When faith is complete it expresses itself in works, the works of righteousness. The Christian religion is predicated upon the promises of God, revealed by the teachings and accomplishments of Jesus. The only way to derive benefit from these promises is by exercise of faith in the person and work of Christ.

Suggestions for the Class

Those who seek to help others find Christ should possess a practical knowledge of the purpose of Christ's coming to the world and be prepared to show from the Scriptures how to be saved.

1. What does it mean to be a Christian?
2. What are the steps one must take to be saved?
3. In what way or ways does Christ save?
4. List and define the different terms used in the New Testament to describe salvation?
5. From what does Christ save? What is selfishness? What is sin? What is sectarianism?
6. For what purpose are we saved? What does it mean to live together with Christ?
7. Interview two or three Christians to find what outstanding thing led them to make their decision for Christ.

Chapter II

WHY WIN OTHERS TO CHRIST?

John Wesley sought Christ for several years before he found him one night at a meeting in a humble cottage on Aldersgate Street in London. Wesley had often wondered why no person offered to help him in his quest. After finding the Lord and having his heart strangely warmed, he wrote the following message to Dr. William Law, his spiritual adviser:

How will you answer to our common Lord that you, Sir, never led me to Christ? Why did I scarcely ever hear you name his name? Why did you never urge me to faith in his blood? Is not Christ the first and the last? If you say that you thought that I had faith already, verily, you do not know me. I beseech you, Sir, by the mercies of God, to consider whether the true reason of your never pressing this salvation upon me was not this—that you never had it yourself!*

This searching inquiry should prompt every person who calls himself Christian to make an honest examination of his own heart.

The Evangelistic Motive

Why speak to another person about Christ? In trying to find an answer, it is well to observe that from the very beginning Christianity has had something in its nature that prompts to witnessing. When Christ was born in Bethlehem, an angel announced to lowly shepherds: "Fear not: for, behold, I bring you good tidings of great joy, which shall be to all people. For

---

*From *The Great Awakening* by Sidney W. Powell. Copyright 1949. Abingdon-Cokesbury Press.

unto you is born this day in the city of David a Savior, which is Christ the Lord" (Luke 2:10-11). In turn, the shepherds "made known abroad the saying which was told them concerning this child" (2:17). Across the centuries since that night those who have found Christ for themselves have been gripped with some mighty compulsion to make him known to others. Nothing has been able to silence their testimony. Some powerful influence, some impelling passion, must motivate them to continue this never-ceasing witness.

Gratitude Makes the Christian Speak

Gratitude to God for his redeeming love and gratitude to that great host of faithful Christians who have brought the gospel message to us imposes upon us a tremendous responsibility to share the witness with others. We have nothing that we have not received by the grace of God and the unselfish devotion of others. How has it happened that the Western world has inherited the gospel while the Eastern world which first received it has been left largely without it? The only answer is that God in providential concern and by his faithful servants has brought it to us.

When Paul and Timothy "assayed to go into Bithynia, the Spirit suffered them not." This is to say that Paul wanted to go east, he tried to go east, but the pressure of God on his heart turned him towards Europe, the home of our ancestors. Thus the gospel has come to us. We would be ingrates indeed, both to God and the long list of witnesses and martyrs who overcame "by the blood of the Lamb and the word of their testimony" if we did not feel any responsibility for making Christ known to others.

Humanity's Desperate Needs Move Us

Those who do not yearn to help others find Christ must be extremely hardhearted, or else they do not really know the woe and suffering of the multitudes without Christ. The physical needs of others alone are enough, if considered seriously, to prompt us to tell them about Christ and his healing power. In America few are far removed from a skilled physician, a trained nurse, and a modern hospital, yet many, many cases are beyond the reach and help of man. Only Christ can restore these persons to health. Someone ought to tell these people about Christ and help them find him.

Consider also the mental needs of people about us. Statistics show that one person out of every twenty-two in our American society spends some time in a mental hospital. This figure does not include the millions of others who have turned to psychiatrists for some form of mental adjustment in recent years. What is wrong with these people? Is it not because they have not learned how to live without fears, tensions, and frustrations in this revolutionary age? They have no peace of mind because their minds are not "stayed on God." These people need to be told how to live by faith in Christ.

If the physical and mental needs of people are great, the spiritual needs are even greater. At least one-half of the American people make no profession of any kind of religion. Of the millions who profess religion many do not know its power to deliver from sin. Whatever value a profession of religion may have, without Christ it leaves the heart empty and void of satisfaction. Only Christ can satisfy the basic yearnings and needs of the human heart. Someone should tell those who have lost their way where to find Christ.

The tragic needs of our American society, not to mention the needs of the people of other lands, present an appeal that constitutes a high motive for helping others find Christ. But though gratitude and sympathy are powerful motives, they are not strong enough to produce the spiritual awakening which this hour demands. Something more dynamic must be found.

3. Christ Within Impels the Christian

A vital experience with God in Christ is the real and adequate motive for helping others find Christ. Let us hear the Apostle Paul, who after finding Christ for himself went forth on missionary enterprises that resulted in turning literally thousands from darkness to light, from sin to salvation, from paganism to Christianity. According to his own testimony, Paul was actuated in his evangelistic work by a personal encounter with Christ. On the Damascus Road something happened to Paul that he never got over. He met Christ face to face. When he rose from the dust into which the heavenly vision had smitten him, he was not the same man. Henceforth there was never any doubt in Paul's mind as to the reality of this experience or the obligation it placed upon him.

Over and over in defense of his apostleship he told the story of his conversion and call. "I have appeared unto thee for this purpose, to make thee a minister and a witness both of these things which thou hast seen, and of those things in the which I will appear unto thee; delivering thee from the people, and from the Gentiles, unto whom now I send thee, to open their eyes, and to turn them from darkness to light, and from the power of Satan unto God, that they may receive forgiveness of sins, and inheritance among them which are sanctified by faith that is in me" (Acts 26:16-18). That settled it for Paul, and ever after, until the time of his death, he had but one burning passion—"to make all men see what is the fellowship of the mystery, which . . . God . . . purposed in Christ Jesus our Lord" (Eph. 3:9-10).

Not only for Paul, but for every Christian, the

motive of evangelism runs back to the nature and purpose of God as revealed by Jesus Christ and apprehended by personal experience through repentance and faith. Those who come to this experience inevitably become evangelistic in spirit and service. The biographies of all the great leaders of the church—Augustine, Francis of Assisi, Luther, Wesley, Edwards, Finney, Moody, Warner, reveal a time when each met Christ face to face. Immediately these men set out to communicate their witness to others.

The same has been true of less-known Christians. We have witnessed it over and over in revival meetings. A new convert rises from the altar, walks down the aisle, puts his hand on a friend's shoulder, gives a simple witness, and brings his friend to Christ. Previously he had not the slightest interest in the spiritual welfare of his friend. Now his first impulse is to bring him to Christ. Why this difference? The only answer is that he has found in Christ an experience so dynamic and constraining that the most natural thing for him to do is to bear witness. He has become a channel of communication for the out-reaching love of God.

Christ's Example Urges Us to Witness

The Christian life consists primarily of two things—being and doing. Emphasis naturally falls first on being. This is where Jesus placed the emphasis. What Christians are determines what they are to do. Here is the true basis of moral obligation. Because Christians are the sons of God, they must live after the fashion of the Son of God. In being, we must be like Jesus; in doing, we must do like Jesus. There is no other standard by which Christians can live. This was the premise from which Jesus reasoned to help his disciples understand what he expected of them. In setting forth his claims, he said: "I am. . . . " Thus he clarified his mission. In pointing out what he expected of his disciples, he said: "Ye are. . . ." Thus he enabled them to see what their responsibility was to be. Let us notice briefly three affirmations he made which clarify this point.

"Ye are the salt of the earth." What salt is to food, Christians are to be to the world. Salt imparts flavor. You can always tell when it is present or absent. It penetrates easily the whole of its environment, without losing its flavor. Salt stimulates thirst. It is a preservative, arresting decay in that to which it is properly applied. These qualities well illustrate what Christians are to be to the world—to impart taste, to create thirst, to penetrate society with Christian influence, and to work constantly for the salvation of the world.

"Ye are the light of the world." The human soul has tremendous possibilities. Christ came as the "true Light, which lighteth every man that cometh into the world" (John 1:9). Of himself he said: "I am the Light of the world." To his disciples he said: "Ye are the light of the world." What light is to life—providing warmth and conditions in which life and vision are possible—that Christians are to be to the world.

Christ Commands Christians to Witness

"Ye shall be witnesses unto me." As Jesus' earthly ministry drew to a close, he commissioned his disciples: "Go ye into all the world and preach the gospel to every creature. He that believeth and is baptized shall be saved; but he that believeth not shall be damned" (Mark 16:15-16). As a final parting promise, he added: "Ye shall receive power, after that the Holy Ghost is come upon you: and ye shall be witnesses unto me both in Jerusalem, and in all Judea, and in Samaria, and unto the uttermost part of the earth" (Acts 1:8). Thus in the clear commands of Jesus and the impelling

dynamic of his Spirit the disciples found the supreme
motivations for helping others find Christ. The Spirit of
Christ is the spirit of witnessing and when his Spirit is
within us we "cannot but speak the things we have
seen and heard" (4:20).

Fear of Failure Moves to Witness

What if we fail? It is no small matter for Christians
not to help others find Christ. Failure here can have
fatal consequences. Christ said, "I am the true vine,
and my Father is the husbandman. Every branch in
me that beareth not fruit he taketh away" (John 15:1-
2). The fruit of one Christian is another Christian. It is
expected of Christians to bring others to Christ, and
when this is not done it jeopardizes one's relationship
with Christ. Bearing fruit is contingent on abiding
constantly in Christ. "He that abideth in me, and I in
him, the same bringeth forth much fruit."

From out of the Old Testament comes God's warning: "Son of man, I have made thee a watchman unto
the house of Israel: therefore hear the word at my
mouth, and give them warning from me. When I say
unto the wicked, Thou shalt surely die; and thou givest
him not warning . . . the same wicked man shall die in
his iniquity; but his blood will I require at thine hand.
Yet if thou warn the wicked, and he turn not from his
wickedness, nor from his wicked way, he shall die in
his iniquity; but thou hast delivered thy soul" (Ezek.
3:17-19). These solemn words declare to those who
know the Word of God and the plight of sinful men the
seriousness of their responsibility. Failure to warn
others of the ultimate end of sin is nothing less than
criminal neglect for which Christians must give an
account before God.

THE EVANGELISTIC MOOD

With what mood shall Christians face their task of helping others find Christ? The answer to this question is vitally important. Failure in winning others is as often traceable to indifference—a lack of a sense of responsibility—as it is to ignorance of how to proceed. Those who help others find Christ must feel deeply the value of a human soul, a compelling need to witness, and a sense of Christ's presence.

Sense the Soul's Real Value

God's evaluation of a human being is supremely higher than that commonly found on earth. The utter lack of appreciation of the soul's value explains the grudging murmur of the elder brother when his lost brother returned. Alas! that so few Christians, though they have tasted salvation themselves, have really entered into God's valuation of a living soul. Were this done the gospel would be given to the world in one generation. Jesus startled the men of his day when he lifted the soul in value above all earthly things. In his estimation, the whole world of material wealth sinks below the worth of any one person.

Successful soul-winning is a passion and an art. It must be a passion before it can be an art. The art of soul-winning can be learned, but the passion for soul-winning must be experienced by "the love of God shed abroad in our hearts by the Holy Ghost." When this passion for souls is in the heart it will find ways of expressing concern for others. God's love in Jesus did, and his love within us will. This passion for souls is what our fathers called "soul burden." Those words describe an attitude of heart and life that must dominate all the activities of the individual Christian and of the church. God's promise is: "He that goeth forth and weepeth, bearing precious seed, shall doubtless come again with rejoicing, bringing his sheaves with him" (Ps. 126: 6).

A missionary came home for a year's furlough, but after three months asked to be sent back to his station. Someone asked, "Why are you going so soon?" He replied, "I can't sleep for thinking of those people." This is the spirit that must possess and motivate each of us if we are to help others find Christ. The Savior's "dying love" must become our "living passion." Christ has committed to his disciples "the ministry of reconciliation . . . and the word of reconciliation." In order to effect this reconciliation we must be moved with compassion for men. Paul explained his matchless career by saying: "I was not disobedient to the heavenly vision." Through the eyes of Christ he caught a vision of the world's need and gave himself in meeting those needs. This is why he was able to say as the curtains of his life dropped: "I am innocent of the blood of all men, for I have not shunned to declare the whole counsel of God."

Feel a Compelling Necessity to Witness

A compelling sense of necessity to witness for Christ because men are going the way of eternal death must motivate the winner of souls. Christians need to feel as did the Apostle Paul: "Necessity is laid upon me; yea, woe is unto me, if I preach not the gospel" (I Cor. 9: 16). The Apostle divided the peoples of the world into two classes: those "in Christ" and those "without Christ." All men outside Christ are lost and need the Christian witness. This truth needs to be emphasized until Christians everywhere are brought to a new conviction of the sinfulness and deadliness of sin. If only we believed what God says about the deadly character of sin, we could not help feeling compelled to "rescue the perishing, care for the dying." We do not deny God's Word; we just do not take it seriously enough at this point.

All about us are the lost, yet few are actually gripped with a strong sense of urgency about their salvation. Our efforts in soul-winning are altogether too spasmodic and transitory. We tend to relegate our witnessing to periods and seasons of the year and fail to realize that the perpetual mood of the Christian must be one of deep concern for the lost. Jesus said: "I must work the works of him that sent me, while it is day: the night cometh, when no man can work" (John 9:4). Christians, too, must work while it is day lest the opportunity to work pass by.

3. Confide in Christ's Presence

A sense of supreme confidence in Christ and his accompanying presence is an essential for the soul winner. The parting promise of Jesus, after he commissioned his first disciples, was: "Lo, I am with you alway, even unto the end of the world" (Matt. 28:20). After Pentecost, the knowledge of Jesus Christ's presence with them and in them enabled the disciples to speak with a certainty and verity that was both convincing and irrefutable. It is no wonder that after a few years these Christians were accused of "turning the world upside down."

Christians today need the baptism of the Holy Spirit to do effective witnessing for Christ. If Jesus thought it expedient for his first disciples to tarry in Jerusalem until they were endued with power from on high before launching their missionary and evangelistic endeavors, can it be less important for his disciples today to be filled with the Spirit's presence and power? "No man can say that Jesus is the Lord, but by the Holy Ghost."

Those who would exalt Christ as Lord most certainly should know whereof they speak. It is the Holy Spirit who "takes the things that are Christ's and makes them known." To assume that we can make disciples for Christ without the consciousness of his presence in our own hearts is nothing short of folly. But when we know Christ and have experienced his grace and power in our own hearts, witnessing for him becomes natural and delightful. "Where the Spirit of the Lord is, there is liberty."

For many people the knowledge of Christ is related to some experience in the past. It is good to retain in one's memory all of the experiences through which Christ has led, but it is far more important that one live daily in the consciousness of His presence. Perhaps one of the chief reasons why the testimony of so many Christians is dull and uninteresting is that it is too far removed from present-day life. It is well to remember the date of one's conversion and sanctification, but it is better to have met "God this morning, while the day was at its best." It is the new assurances that come to us daily that keep the soul singing and witnessing.

The Evangelistic Message

Another reason for helping others find Christ is found in the gospel itself. It is "good news" of such kind and quality that it demands being told, as Dr. William Newton Clarke has so ably said:

The intention to conquer is characteristic of the gospel. That was the aim of its youth when it went forth among the religions that then surrounded it, and with this aim it must enter any field in which old religions are encumbering the religious nature of man. It cannot conquer except in love, but in love it intends to conquer. It means to fill the world.*

One day during the last week of Jesus' earthly ministry, he left Jerusalem and sat down on a mountainside overlooking the city. There his disciples inquired concerning some of his pronouncements about the destruction of the Temple. They asked: "When shall these things be? And what shall be the sign of thy coming, and of the end of the world?" In his answer he told them of false prophets to come, of wars and rumors of wars, of famines, pestilences, earthquakes, sorrows, afflictions, persecutions, offenses, increase of iniquity, and coldness of love. Then he added, to remind them of their true mission: "This gospel of the kingdom shall be preached in all the world for a witness unto all nations; and then shall the end come" (Matt. 24:14).

Several questions come to mind as we ponder seriously these words of Jesus expressing faith in the continued witness of the gospel regardless of things to come. What is the gospel? What objectives did Jesus have in mind to accomplish through the witness of the gospel? How will this gospel be preached to all the world? Let us consider these questions in order:

1. What Is the Gospel?

Jesus identified his message as "this gospel of the kingdom," to set it apart from any other form of teaching and to relate it to his own life and teaching. This is indeed significant, for the English word "gospel" comes from the Anglo-Saxon word *godspel,* which meant *god-story,* or good tidings. The gospel, then, is God's story as it was presented to the world by his Son Jesus

---

*From *The Sound of Trumpets* by Arthur J. Moore. Copyright, Abingdon-Cokesbury Press.

Christ. In short, the gospel is "the story of how the Son of God became the Son of man that the sons of men might become sons of God." In the original Greek of the New Testament, so we are told by scholars, the root word is *euangelion,* from which come our words evangel, evangelism, and evangelist. The evangelistic message is the evangel, the good news, the gospel.

Paul describes the gospel as "the power of God unto salvation to every one that believeth" (Rom. 1:16). To him, the gospel included the whole scheme of God's redemptive plan as expressed through the life, death, resurrection, and mediation of Christ. Three great emphases of the gospel appear in Paul's epistles: blood redemption, bodily resurrection, and the return of Christ. Blood redemption is effected by faith in the atonement of Christ; bodily resurrection is our hope since Christ brought "life and immortality to light"; the return of Christ is the consummation of all earthly things, at which time all men will "stand before God in judgment."

What Are the Gospel Objectives?

For what purpose has Christ ordained that "this gospel . . . shall be preached in all the world"? At least four answers are forthcoming from a study of the Gospel record.

The first objective of the gospel is *the salvation of the lost.* This was the purpose of Christ's coming into the world, as has been already discussed. The gospel presents the story of what God has done to effect man's salvation and what man must do to be saved.

A second objective of the gospel is *the establishment of the church.* During the second year of his ministry Jesus announced to his disciples: "I will build my church, and the gates of hell shall not prevail against it." In the Acts of the Apostles the church is declared to be a living reality to which God added members daily. Having elders and laity, meeting together for worship, holding conferences and making decisions on points of doctrine and practice, sending forth missionaries, collecting funds for the poor, the early church maintained a strong witness for Christ. Paul declares that Christ is the head of the church; in turn, the church is the body of Christ, the habitation of Christ's Spirit, and his bride. The purpose of the church is to make "all men see what is . . . the eternal purpose which he [God] has purposed in Christ Jesus our Lord" (Eph. 3:9-11).

All who repent of their sins and believe the gospel —all "whom he has purchased with his own blood"— make up the membership of the church. By the gospel Christians have fellowship with each other and share a common objective—helping others find Christ. It is natural and right that those who accept Christ as Lord and Savior should meet together for fellowship and worship, and to unite their efforts in evangelism. In and through the church Christ carries forward his work of redemption in the world.

A third objective of the gospel is *the restoration of the home to its original sanctity*. When he was asked by the Pharisees: "Is it lawful for a man to put away his wife for every cause?" Jesus reminded them of God's original plan for the human family. To this they answered that Moses in the Law made provision for divorce. Jesus replied: "Moses because of the hardness of your hearts suffered you to put away your wives: but from the beginning it was not so" (Matt. 19:8). He went beyond the Law of Moses and focused attention on God's original plan. Through the gospel he revealed a pattern of behavior, a basis for human relationships, that makes divorce unnecessary and undesirable. The gospel is designed to restore human personality to its original pattern of life, the home to its original sanctity, and society to a fellowship of redemption.

No other institution in American society has been so severely attacked in recent years as the home. At no other point in our civilization is moral collapse more evident. In 1884 there was only one divorce to every thirty-two marriages. The general public in those days attached a moral taboo to those who divorced and all but ostracized them from society. Fifty years later, in 1934, the ratio between marriage and divorce was cut in half, one divorce to every sixteen marriages. Along about this time there swept across the nation like a prairie fire a teaching suggesting trial marriages on the basis of biological selection and compatibility. The teaching took root immediately in man's carnal nature. By 1940, or within a six-year period, the divorce rate increased until there was one divorce to every eight marriages.

Then came World War II with its accompanying evils. Millions of American youth entered hastily into marriage and then were absented from their companions from one to five years. With the end of the war in 1945 there came a rush to the divorce courts which skyrocketed the rate to one divorce to every three marriages. Such is the appalling condition within the American home. Never before has there been so great need for some kind of "cement" or "cohesive" to hold life together. That cement and cohesive are found only in the gospel of Christ.

The final objective of the gospel to be discussed here is *the preparation of men's hearts for the world to come.* This objective is not unlike the first. But Christ has so much to say about the end of the world that

it is deemed expedient to say something about it here.
It is here that Christians find one of their greatest in-
centives for living.

Christ made it clear that "the word that I have
spoken, the same shall judge him in the last day"
(John 12:48). When he returns to judge the world, all
that are in "the graves shall hear his voice, and shall
come forth; they that have done good, unto the resurrection of life; and they that have done evil, unto the
resurrection of damnation" (5:28-29). The test on that
day will be whether man has accepted or rejected Jesus
Christ and whether those who have accepted him have
lived in obedience to his gospel. On that day, writes
Paul, "God shall judge the secrets of men by Jesus
Christ according to my gospel" (Rom. 2:16).

The ultimate test of discipleship, according to Jesus,
will be whether or not we have fed the hungry, welcomed the stranger, clothed the needy, visited the sick
and imprisoned, and kept the whole will of God. If so,
then we shall hear his words: "Come, ye blessed of my
Father, inherit the kingdom prepared for you from the
foundation of the world." If not so, we shall hear instead: "Depart from me, ye cursed, into everlasting
fire, prepared for the devil and his angels." Then Christ
will add: "Inasmuch as ye have done it unto one of the
least of these my brethren, ye have done it unto me.
. . . Inasmuch as ye did it not to one of the least of
these, ye did it not to me" (Matt. 25:40-45). The
only way whereby we can improve our own standing
before Christ is by helping others; the only service we
can render to him is for others.

How Preach the Gospel in All the World?

What is preaching? The preaching of the gospel
embraces every legitimate method of witnessing that
can be used in extending the message to others. Jesus

did not say exactly how the witness should be given, but he declared that the gospel should be preached— that is, heralded forth for others to hear it and be brought under its power and influence. He left it to Christians in every age to find their own way of getting the message to all the world.

By the Holy Spirit God bestows spiritual gifts upon those who prepare their hearts by full surrender to do his will; the gift bestowed by the Spirit of God determines the place one is to fill in witnessing to the gospel. "There are differences of administrations. . . . There are diversities of operations. . . . But the manifestation of the Spirit is given to every man to profit withal" (I Cor. 12:5-7). Christians are to "covet earnestly the best gifts" and more especially the gift of love.

God calls some to the special task of preaching. "How shall they hear without a preacher? And how shall they preach, except they be sent?" (Rom. 10:14-15). Those who are divinely called to this work should endeavor to preach, not "with enticing words of man's wisdom, but in demonstration of the Spirit and of power" (I Cor. 2:4). When preaching is done in this fashion, whether behind a pulpit or in an open field, it has tremendous power to bring men to repentance and faith. It has pleased God "by the foolishness of preaching to save them that believe."

Suggestions for the Class

The New Testament makes it clear that motive determines the moral quality of action. Christians ought to pray; but for their prayer to be acceptable with God, their motives must be right. Christians ought to give alms, but not to be seen of men. This principle applies to everything a Christian does. For this reason the motives that impel Christians to witness need to be carefully analyzed.

1. Evaluate the five motives discussed in this study of

why Christians ought to help others. Which motive seems to you most impelling and vital?

2. How can the Christian more intensely sense the lostness of humanity?

3. What motivated the Apostle Paul in his evangelistic and missionary endeavors? How do you account for his great accomplishments in such a short length of time?

4. What does Christ expect of Christians? How did Jesus point out to his first disciples what he expected of them? What is the true basis of moral obligation?

5. What do we mean when we say that Christians must have an evangelistic mood?

6. What are the four objectives of the gospel discussed in this study? Can you think of other objectives?

7. How can the home and the church work more closely **together?**

Chapter III

HOW JESUS WON OTHERS

In every realm of life where influence is to be exerted the study of people is important. It is most vital to success in helping others find Christ. No task is more **sacred, and** the person who does it needs divine help. Each person is a unique personality and no one can properly be classified as to type or member of a certain class. No person can be fitted neatly into a pigeonhole designed for someone else. Whatever approach is made must be adapted to the particular person being sought.

In our attempt to help others find Christ it is well to remember that we are moving in the realm of God's work. Conversion, in reality, is the work of the Spirit of God. In the realm of the spiritual, techniques and methods may seem out of place, yet they are indispensable. God himself has observable ways of reaching the soul, and ours is the task of watching and learning how God works. From this observation we may map out certain principles of procedure. Certainly such observation will reveal an endless variety of Christian experiences and of God's working.

We can be most grateful that God has given us the example of his Son to guide us in this work. Not only did Jesus commission us to "go . . . make disciples"; he set before us his own example of how to do it. Someone has observed: "The Master's plan of evangelism is still the master plan of evangelism." This is indeed true, as we shall find out. By studying the persons Jesus helped, the principles he followed, the techniques and appeals he used, we can derive invaluable help in our own witnessing task.

Persons Jesus Won

Jesus highly personalized his ministry. The greater portion of his sayings that have been preserved for us are statements that he made to individuals. A man seeking personal fame or notoriety would never have used such poor judgment as to waste his most brilliant and profound conceptions on one or a few persons. The greatest truth Jesus made known about God, he revealed at Jacob's well to a woman of questionable character; the most significant thing he said about the new birth was spoken to one man who came to him by night. Even the Sermon on the Mount was not delivered to the multitude, but to his disciples.

Christ won all kinds of people—rich men, poor men, beggarmen, thieves, d o c t o r s, lawyers, merchants, priests. Though he was constantly surrounded with the masses, yet he was particularly interested in the individual and did all he could to help each—one by one. Without attempting to classify the cases, a study of the Gospels reveals the following examples of his contacts with individuals:

1. Andrew, John, and Peter (John 1:35-42)
2. Philip and Nathanael (John 1:43-51)
3. Nicodemus (John 3:1-15)
4. The woman of Samaria (John 4:1-42)
5. The nobleman (John 4:46-54)
6. The call of Simon, Andrew, James, and John (Luke 5:1-11)
7. A leper (Mark 1:40-45)
8. A paralytic borne by four (Mark 2:1-12)
9. The call of Matthew (Mark 2:13-17)
10. The infirm man at Bethesda (John 5:1-15)
11. The man with a withered hand (Luke 6:6-11)
12. The centurion (Luke 7:1-10)
13. The widow of Nain (Luke 7:11-17)

14. The sinful woman in Simon's house (Luke 7:37-50)
15. The Gadarene demoniac (Mark 5:1-20)
16. Jairus and his family (Mark 5:21-43)
17. The woman with the issue of blood (Mark 5:25-34)
18. The two blind men (Matt. 9:27-31)
19. The dumb demoniac (Matt. 9:32-34)
20. The Syrophoenician woman (Matt. 15:21-28)
21. The deaf and dumb man (Mark 7:32-37)
22. The blind man near Bethsaida (Mark 8:22-26)
23. The demoniac boy (Mark 9:14-29)
24. The woman taken in adultery (John 8:1-11)
25. The three would-be disciples (Luke 9:51-62)
26. The lawyer (Luke 10:25-37)
27. The woman bowed double (Luke 13:10-17)
28. The rich young ruler (Matt. 19:16-22)
29. The blind men near Jericho (Mark 10:46-52)
30. Zaccheus (Luke 19:1-10)
31. Judas Iscariot (Luke 22:21, 47-48; John 13:21-30; Matt. 27:3-5)
32. Pilate (John 18—19; Luke 23:1-25)
33. Herod (Luke 23:6-12)
34. The two thieves (Luke 23:32-43)

A study of these instances will show that Jesus used an infinite variety of ways in ministering to the needs of individuals. He never approached two persons in exactly the same way, nor employed the same method twice. His interviewing was informal, natural, spontaneous, and frequently interrupted. He understood the needs of man and always spoke directly of the thing needful for right relations with God. His wayside ministries are especially illuminating, for he was never too busy to care for the problems of the individual soul. He handled each case with unequaled skill, and he remains to this day the ideal example to all who would do personal work.

PRINCIPLES JESUS FOLLOWED

When Jesus was handed the scroll in the synagogue at Nazareth, at the outset of his ministry, he selected the passage which reads: "The Spirit of the Lord is upon me, because he hath anointed me to preach the gospel to the poor; he hath sent me to heal the broken-hearted, to preach deliverance to the captives, and recovering of sight to the blind, to set at liberty them that are bruised, to preach the acceptable year of the Lord" (Luke 4:18-19). This passage became the preamble of his life and work. From the outset of his ministry, Jesus felt that his mission was to relieve human suffering whether physical, mental, moral, or spiritual. Our purpose here is to study the principles he used in fulfilling this mission.

Jesus Took Interest in People

Christ took a personal interest in people and their problems. No person was beyond the scope of his concern. Though there were endless numbers of people who sought his help, he always had time for each individual and his needs. As has been pointed out already, he helped all kinds of people. In doing so, Jesus ignored all the barriers that existed in his day.

Christ enlisted Simon the Zealot as a disciple, setting aside political distinction (Luke 6:15). He dined with Zaccheus, setting aside class distinction (19:5). He conversed with the woman of Samaria, setting aside sex distinctions (John 4:27). He responded to the appeal of the Syrophoenician woman, setting aside race distinction (Mark 7:26). He extolled the faith of the centurion, setting aside national distinction (Matt. 8:10). He allowed the woman who was a sinner to touch him, setting aside reputational distinction (Luke 7:39). He praised the poor widow who gave her mite, setting aside economic distinction (Mark 12:43). He washed his disciple's feet, setting aside the master-servant distinction (John 13:14). He rebuked his disciples for their intolerance toward that follower who was not of the twelve, setting aside religious distinction (Mark 9:39). He enjoyed the company of children, setting aside age distinction (Matt. 21:15-16).*

*From *That They May Have Life,* by Daniel T. Niles. Copyright, 1951, The Student Volunteer Movement.

Jesus Knew What People Thought

Christ gave priority to the dominant interests of people. He began with people where he found them and used the familiar to illustrate what they could become. He talked in terms of a sower going forth to sow, the building of a house, the catching of fish, the cultivation of a vineyard, the establishment of a home, the finding a buried treasure, a father's love for his wayward boy. All of these were of practical interest to the people who came to him. He used these things as avenues of approach to talk about man's relationship to God.

An interesting study of how Jesus used a dominant interest as an approach to a moral conflict is the story of his conversation with the Samaritan woman at Jacob's well. He opened the conversation at the woman's point of interest—water. She had come with her waterpot to the well. Jesus asked her for a drink. Immediately she began to unveil the conflicts in her life. The first was the cultural conflict: She was a Samaritan, Jesus was a Jew, yet he had spoken to her. Jesus assured her that if she had asked him for water, he would have given her living water. Another conflict arose: the Jacob and Jesus conflict. "Are you greater than our father Jacob, who gave us the well?" Jesus assured the woman of his willingness to give her "a well of water springing up to everlasting life." She asked for this water. Jesus instructed her to call her husband. She excused herself by saying, "I have no husband." Jesus brought her face to face with the moral problem in her life. Another conflict appeared: Where is God to be worshiped? in this mountain or in Jerusalem? Jesus drove home the answer: "Woman, believe me, the hour cometh . . . and now is, when the true worshipers shall worship the Father in spirit and in truth: for the Father seeketh such to worship him. God is a Spirit: and they that worship him must worship him in spirit and in truth" (John 4:21-24). Thus Jesus progressed from her dominant interest—water—to her basic need—salvation.

Jesus Emphasized Faith

Jesus led people to think about what they believed, not what they doubted. Over and over Jesus emphasized the importance of faith. Some of his most characteristic words were "Fear not." "Be not afraid," "Have faith in God." Everywhere he found faith he honored and praised it. He held forth invitations to the distressed and oppressed that appealed to faith: "Come," "Seek," "Enter," "Believe." Whenever he was confronted with honest doubt, as in the case of Thomas, Jesus met it with convincing evidence. At the same time he talked of the greater blessing of faith that does not require physical evidences to support it. He talked in terms of the possibilities of a little faith, "the size of a grain of mustard seed." For those who could believe, he held forth absolutely limitless promises: "All things are possible to him that believeth"; "What things soever ye desire when ye pray, believe that ye receive them, and ye shall have them." It was thus that he sought to set men free from needless worry and anxiety, aimlessness and hopelessness.

Jesus Expected People to Think

Jesus helped men find the answer to their own questions and problems. The teachings of Christ were revolutionary on many points. He challenged conditions as they were (status quo) and asked questions. He answered questions by asking questions. A case in point is the lawyer who raised the question, "Who is my neighbor?" Jesus told the story of the Good Sa-

maritan, then asked: "Which now of these three, think-
est thou, was neighbor unto him that fell among the
thieves?" The answer was obvious and when the
lawyer called it rightly, Jesus added: "Go, and do thou
likewise."

Another day the Pharisees and Herodians asked: "Is
it lawful to pay tribute unto Caesar, or not?" Jesus
called for a piece of tribute money and asked: "Whose
is this image and superscription?" "Caesar's," they
said. Then Jesus left them to decide what belongs to
God and what belongs to Caesar. Some questions he
answered directly, as in the case of the rich young
ruler. He never left any uncertainty in the minds of
his inquirers about their moral responsibility.

Jesus Gave the Scriptures Prominence

To the Sadducees, Jesus said: "Ye err, not knowing
the scriptures." He could say this, for he knew the
Scriptures. He used the Scriptures in overcoming his
temptations in the wilderness and in teaching the
people. His interpretation of Scripture differed con-
siderably from that of the religious leaders of his day,
and because of this he encountered some sharp conflicts. He translated the Word of God into life and
spirit, fulfilling it in his own life.

Jesus Knew What Was in Man

The Lord confronted people with a true picture of
their moral and spiritual condition. He never made
discipleship easy in order to attract followers. In fact,
he seemed at times to take special pains to make
discipleship difficult. He let those who would follow
him know what his expectations were beforehand. He
talked in terms of self-denial, forsaking all, taking up a
cross, and of tribulations. Confession of sin, repentance,

forgiveness of others, reconciliation with others, restitution, all were held forth by him as requisites for
salvation.

Jesus condemned prayer, fasting, and giving alms,
when the motive was to obtain praise from men. He
reasoned that the quality of an action is always determined by the desire that motivates it. The bitterest
words that Jesus ever spoke were in denunciation of
hypocrisy and insincerity in religion. At no time did
he compromise with sin. He stuck to his purpose having
counted the cost. Even when his closest friends tried
to swerve him from his loyalty to truth, he rebuked
them sternly, saying: "Get thee behind me, Satan." He
insisted that everything must be sacrificed for the
kingdom of God.

Jesus Recognized Personal Responsibility

Jesus did not let his failures discourage him. He was
not 100 per cent successful in his work. There were
some who refused his help. Still others failed to meet
his demands for discipleship. Only a few recognized
his true identity. In every case it was the attitude of the
individual that determined the success or failure of
Jesus' efforts. His attitude was one of helpfulness; at
all times he was able, willing, and ready to help, but
he did not always find a willing response to his help. In
Nazareth "he could there do no mighty work . . . because
of their unbelief" (Mark 6:5-6). No fault can be found
with Jesus, the methods he used, or his understanding
of human needs. His success was always contingent
on the attitude and response of people towards him.
You cannot help people who refuse to be helped. The
most distressing circumstance Jesus had to face was
the stubborn unbelief he found in the hearts of people
who boasted of having faith in God. "When the Son of

man cometh, shall he find faith on the earth?" (Luke 18:8).

The Gospels—Matthew, Mark, Luke, and John— abound in stories about Jesus and the methods he used in bringing his witness to others. Matthew describes him as going about all Galilee, "teaching in their synagogues, and preaching the gospel of the kingdom, and healing all manner of sickness and all manner of disease among the people." Continuing, he records that "his fame went throughout all Syria: and they brought unto him all sick people . . . with divers diseases and torments, and those which were possessed, . . . lunatic, . . . palsy; and he healed them" (Matt. 4:23-24). "Teaching . . . preaching . . . healing" were the principal methods he used. He taught to clarify men's thinking and enlighten their minds; he preached to stir their emotions and to move their wills; and he healed that they might have maximum use of their bodies in service for God. Here we shall study some of the techniques he used in bringing help to people.

Jesus Used Personal Interviews

Jesus' evangelistic efforts began late one afternoon following his baptism and temptation in the wilderness, as he walked alongside the Jordan River, near where John the Baptist was standing with two of his disciples. John saw him and said concerning him: "Behold the Lamb of God, which taketh away the sin of the world." Two of John's disciples, Andrew and John, heard his words and followed after Jesus. When Jesus asked them, "What seek ye?" they answered, "Where dwellest thou?" Jesus invited them to "come and see." They spent the rest of the day in intimate conversation with Jesus and came away with the deep conviction that he was the Messiah. Andrew sought his brother Simon and brought him to Jesus with a testimony that was purely personal and convincing.

All during his ministry Jesus was sought out by persons who wanted personal interviews with him. Some desired of him an answer to some of life's most difficult problems. Not a few came to him for healing for themselves or for a child or servant. No doubt, some came for the sole purpose of being able to tell others that they had seen him and talked with him. Though Jesus was constantly pressed upon by the crowds, he always found time for the individual and his personal problems and questions.

The modern emphasis on psychology and personal work has led to a new appreciation of the insights and methods of Jesus. Ministers and religious leaders are increasingly studying and seeking to follow the example of Jesus at this point of personal work. There is no more effective way to bring comfort to the distressed, guidance to the bewildered, peace to the troubled, and salvation to the lost than the person-to-person, heart-to-heart conversation.

Jesus Enlisted and Trained Others

Jesus did not work alone. Early in his ministry he chose twelve men and ordained them to be apostles. These men were chosen from all walks of life, a motley group indeed—fishermen, tax collectors, merchants. They forsook all and followed Jesus wherever he went and stood ready to do his every command. When others forsook Jesus and he questioned their loyalty to him, the Twelve replied, "Lord, to whom shall we go? Thou hast the words of eternal life." Such was their evaluation of Jesus and their devotion to him. Though they did not always understand him or his teachings, yet they willingly subjected themselves to his disciplines and dedicated their lives to his service. At his command they went out to preach the gospel of his kingdom and heal the sick.

During the second year of his ministry, Jesus called seventy other disciples and sent them forth to witness for him. "The Lord appointed other seventy also, and sent them two and two before his face into every city and place, whither he himself would come" (Luke 10:1). As with the Twelve the work of the Seventy was definitely assigned to them. They were to "heal the sick . . . and say to them, the kingdom of God is come nigh unto you." Their witness was to be given person to person, house to house, and city to city. Something of their work and successes is recorded in Luke 10:17.

Jesus gave specific instruction to the Twelve and the Seventy before he sent them out to witness to others. He told them where to go, what to do when they arrived, and how to conduct themselves if their witness was not received. He paired the witnesses two and two and sent them "into every town and city where he was about to come." He instructed them to find in each place a lodging from which to carry on their mission in order to conserve time and reach the greatest possible number of people. As evidence of the authenticity of their witness he gave them his power to heal the sick. He enjoined them to live sacrificially, take along no extra money, food, or clothing, and to trust in God for the supply of their needs. Should they encounter opposition or rejection in any city, they were to continue their mission in other places.

Jesus Exalted the Home and Church

Jesus found in the home and in the synagogue two centers of evangelistic interest. He made a path between the home and the church and the church and the home. Some of the most gracious incidents left to us from the life of Jesus center in someone's home. At

the beginning of his ministry he attended a wedding
in Cana of Galilee and there performed his first mir-
acle. Throughout his ministry he often entered homes
to heal, to eat, and to teach. Matthew, after his call to
follow Jesus, opened his house and invited in his
friends to fellowship with the Lord. "As Jesus sat at
meat in his house, many publicans and sinners sat also
together with Jesus and his disciples: for there were
many, and they followed him" (Mark 2:15).

Jesus invited himself to the house of Zaccheus; the
crowd murmured, but Zaccheus got saved. Four men
took the roof off a house where Jesus sat teaching, in
order to get a paralyzed man to him for healing and
salvation. He told the demoniac of Gadara, after he
had healed him, and the man had requested that he
might follow with Jesus and his disciples: "Go home,
and tell what good things the Lord hath done for you."
The home of Lazarus, Mary, and Martha was often
blessed with Jesus' presence. He entered the home
of Jairus, ruler of a synagogue, and raised his
daughter from the dead.

"He taught them in their synagogue" is a statement
frequently found in the Gospels. Synagogues for
teaching religion and worship had been developed in
all the towns and cities of Palestine. Jesus found in
them an opportunity to confront the people with the
message of the gospel, and he did so. It was here that
he encountered some of his strongest opposition because he disregarded the religious traditions of the
Pharisees and Sadducees and proceeded to meet
human needs even on the Sabbath. Probably one reason
why we have no record of the early Christians' erecting
places of worship is that they followed closely the
example of Jesus in using the synagogues already established as preaching and teaching centers.

Jesus Went Where the People Were

When Jesus began his ministry he went where the people were; as he continued his ministry the people came where he was. The multitudes followed him wherever he went. He taught them from the mountainside, in the desert, on the seashore, in the Temple, and in the market places. His ministry in the open country was unique. On at least two occasions he performed miracles of providing food for the crowds rather than sending them away hungry and untaught.

No person has crowded so much into so few years as did Jesus. He had but one all-consuming passion—the reaching of people with the witness of the gospel. In doing so, he used a variety of methods and techniques, some old, some new, but all enhanced by his skill. He knew the value and importance of human personality and sought to redeem it for service to God. There were times when he witnessed directly and with clarity, when there could be no mistaking the meaning of what he said. At other times, especially when he was being opposed by the Pharisees and Sadducees, he veiled his message in parables and left it to the people to construct their own interpretation of his words. He refused to use any method that was incongruous with his ultimate purpose—that of bringing men face to face with their moral responsibility to both God and man. His techniques and methods remain unexcelled to this day.

APPEALS JESUS MADE

In winning others to God the important thing is to bring them to a decision. Without it, there can be no conversion experience. Christ always taught with the view of bringing the other person to a point of decision. The propositions he presented were inescapable.

The appeals he made are basic, and any person desiring to help others find their way into the life of the Spirit cannot afford to be ignorant of these appeals and how to use them effectively. Let us here consider some of the appeals Jesus made.

Jesus Appealed to Men's Insights

Central in all the appeals Jesus made was the appeal to the high spiritual insights of which man is capable. To the hearts of his disciples he pressed the question: "Who do you say that I am?" And of the Pharisees he asked: "What think ye of Christ?" He knew that what men thought about him was most important. This is the supreme question of life and of death. What he was he knew man must become to have fellowship with God. He knew what he was, what man was, and how to bridge the chasm between what man was and what man could be. Some did recognize God in Jesus; others did not, but unto as many as did recognize and receive him "to them gave he power to become the sons of God."

Jesus Appealed to Conscience

To the Pharisees who brought to him the woman taken in adultery, tempting him, Jesus said: "He that is without sin among you, let him cast the first stone at her." And they, "being convicted by their own conscience, went out one by one." By both his person and his teachings Jesus probed deeply into the consciences of men. In his presence, Peter fell on his knees, crying: "Depart from me, for I am a sinful man." The demons within the man of Gadara cried out: "We know who thou art, thou holy Son of God; why hast thou come to torment us before our time?" Jesus did torment men with the consciousness of their sin. But yet, if men would accept his words, he came not into the world to "condemn the world; but that the world through him might be saved" (John 3:17). His purpose was not to intensify the consciousness of guilt but to purge the conscience from guilt and sin. He made the knowledge of sin the antecedent of salvation.

Jesus Appealed to Reason

"What think ye?" was the question with which he prefaced many of his parables. He recognized man's capacity to reason, and so he confronted man with something to reason out. Knowing that whatever gets a man's thoughts eventually gets the man, Jesus endeavored to direct man's thoughts toward God. He made man think about God, about himself, about his brother, and about his eternal destiny. No one has made men think more than did Jesus; no person has ever given men so much to think about! It was while the two disciples of Emmaus, after the resurrection, communed "together and reasoned, Jesus himself drew near" (Luke 24:15). He always draws near to men who reason about him.

Jesus Appealed to Faith

One man, whose son was possessed with an evil spirit, begged Jesus: "If thou canst do anything, have compassion on us, and help us." Jesus put the responsibility squarely on the man, saying: "If thou canst believe, all things are possible to him that believeth" (Mark 9:22-23). Jesus knew that every man had the capacity to believe, and he worked to increase faith to an unlimited degree. Over against the fear, frustration, and uncertainty which he found in the hearts of men, he put faith as the solution to all of life's problems. He did not try to lead men to believe the impossible, but he did try to anchor men's faith in God with whom all things are possible. He helped men discover and live by the moral and spiritual laws written into the constitution of their being. He presented tangible evidences as a foundation for faith. On one occasion he proposed to the Pharisees who questioned him: "If I do not the works of my Father, believe me not. But if I do, though ye believe not me, believe the works: that ye may know, and believe, that the Father is in me, and I in him" (John 10:37-38).

Jesus Appealed to Need for Useful Action

"Go, thou, and do likewise" was his direction to the lawyer who asked who his neighbor was. Jesus said that a man who heard his sayings and did them was a wise man, while the man who heard them and did them not was a foolish man. And he left it to every man to determine his own classification. In his parables of stewardship and talents he made it clear that ability is the measure of responsibility. He made it clear that to know constitutes a command to do. To his disciples he said: "Happy are ye, if ye know these things and do them." And again he said: "If any man will do his will, he shall know." He made knowledge a measure of obedience and obedience a source of knowledge. He brought into the lives of those who became his disciples a new motive and incentive for work. It was "for my sake."

Jesus Appealed to Man's Sense of Value

"What is a man profited if he shall gain the whole world, and lose his own soul?" Jesus did not deal with trivialities. When he focused attention on a matter it was because of its supreme importance. And he did raise the question of the value of a human soul. He left one part of the equation for man to determine for himself: "What shall a man give in exchange for his soul?" "How much is a man better than a sheep?" He left every man to set a price on his own head, yet he warned that the way to save life is to lose it in service to others and to God.

Jesus Appealed to the Fear of Retribution

His ultimatum to all men was: "Except ye repent, ye shall all likewise perish." In presenting his claims to men he made definite the advantages of accepting them and he made positive the dangers of rejecting them. He had more to say about hell than he did about heaven. At first thought, this may seem to contradict his gospel of love. Not so, for Jesus knew where sin was leading the human family, and he was determined to do something about it.

But since man is a moral being, with freedom of will and decision, Jesus could not effect a plan of salvation that would override the free choice of man. What he did was to provide for man's salvation through the gift of his love and then work to effect that salvation in man's life. But if man refuses to be saved, then the inevitable consequence of his own choice determines his destiny. "Repent ye, and believe the gospel" Jesus set forth as man's alternative to continuing in sin. "He that believeth and is baptized shall be saved; but he that believeth not shall be damned" (Mark 16:16). Man damns his own soul by his own unbelief and rejection of the gospel. Witnesses must set this matter squarely before those who believe not the gospel.

SUGGESTIONS FOR THE CLASS

Jesus' way of helping others is unique. In his example we find a true pattern for the whole of human behavior. We cannot rise to his level of perfection, but we can move in that direction. No person can pattern his life after Jesus without attaining great living. Principles have been discussed in this lesson, which, if applied to life, will produce results today.

1. Read the scriptural references concerning the persons Jesus helped and note carefully just how the help was given.

2. What principles did Jesus follow in helping others? How did he help people help themselves?

3. What techniques did Christ use? Can you find a pattern of organization in his use of helpers?

4. What two centers close to the people did Jesus use? How can such centers be used today?

5. Why is the personal approach method of winning others so effective?

6. In what different ways can we apply the appeals made by Jesus in leading others to decision? What appeal would you say is the most compelling? Why?

7. The next time you sit in a church service where an appeal is made for the acceptance of Christ, analyze it and measure its effectiveness in bringing others to a decision. What appeal would you say is most frequently used?

Chapter IV

WAYS OF WINNING OTHERS

Some years ago when the Prince of Wales, who later became King Edward VIII, was visiting in this country, he was entertained in the home of a man living in Washington, D.C. On the following Christmas, the Prince decided to send his host a card. Not remembering his host's exact address, he put only his name, his city, and U.S.A. on the card and placed it in the mail. In due time the card was returned to England, with the stamped memorandum: "Cannot locate: Insufficient Address." Upon receiving the card, the Prince wrote in bold letters across it: "Find this man!" Then he attached his royal signature and sent the card back to America. The card was delivered!

Over nineteen hundred years ago, Jesus Christ, the Prince of glory, came into this world. While here, he lived a most humble life, identifying himself with sinful humanity. For a little more than three years he preached and taught about the kingdom of God, healed the sick and cast out devils. Then he was put to death on a cross outside the city of Jerusalem. Three days later he rose from the dead, appeared to his disciples for forty days, then ascended to heaven. Just before his departure from the world, however, he gathered a company of about five hundred disciples about him, and said: "Go ye therefore, and make disciples of all nations." That commission is now binding upon all Christians.

"Go make disciples of all nations." The person to whom this command is directed is YOU. Christ would have every Christian understand it in this manner. It is an individual and personal directive, and cannot be obeyed by proxy. The command does not read "send ye." In fulfilling this commission every single Christian has his full measure of responsibility. It must be borne individually and to the extent of one's ability. The work cannot be relegated to someone else. Each Christian must tell his own story or it will not be told. The command is both individual and universal; the personal pronoun *you* is both singular and plural. It is only when you "win the one next to you, and I win the one next to me" that the command is fulfilled. It is both "Go into all the world" and "Find this man!"

"Bring him to me" was the request of Jesus to his disciples, when they met a case too difficult for them to handle. (See Matthew 17:17.) It is his request of his disciples today. How to do it is the problem. Here we shall begin a study of some practical ways of bringing others to Christ.

PERSONAL EVANGELISM

Personal evangelism, stated simply, is one person helping another person find Christ. This definition presupposes that the first person is a Christian while the second is not. But how can this task of helping others find Christ be done most effectively? How can one give his witness convincingly? Let us here note ten helps to successful soul-winning.

Tell What Christ Has Done for You

Learn to tell your own story with skill and interest. Effective witnesses for Christ in every age have made large use of the first personal pronoun—not because they have wished to set themselves up as examples of the finished product of Christ, but because they have not been able to escape the responsibility of sharing their personal experience with others. The Apostle Paul was a master here. In Jerusalem before the infuriated Jews and in Caesarea before King Agrippa he defended his apostleship by giving his personal testimony. His epistles abound with personal affirmations: "I know on whom I have believed"; "That which I have received of the Lord Jesus Christ I give unto you"; "I am not ashamed of the gospel of Christ"; "I live, yet not I, but Christ liveth in me." No person can fully calculate what these glowing words have meant to saints of all succeeding ages.

The experience of Christ in the soul is so deeply personal and sacred that one often hesitates to talk about it. Like the love of husband and wife, the relationship with Christ is so peculiarly a part of that inner self where one treasures the most precious verities of life, that the temptation is to shrink from exposing it to the gaze of others. Many Christians, like many husbands and wives, fail at this very point. Love, both divine and human, needs expression. The person who experiences Christ in his soul must find some tangible way to give expression to that love or its glow will fade away. One of the best ways to keep a home together is for husband and wife to find ways of expressing their love to each other and affirming it constantly before others. The same is true of the Christian; sharing one's love for Christ in testimony to others helps to keep one's love for Christ intense and warm. "One loving heart can set another heart aflame."

See in Each Person One for Whom Christ Died

Regard every person as your own responsibility. Door to door salesmen have a slogan which goes: "Every person a prospect!" But the Christian cannot stop with merely looking upon the other person as a prospect—in a most real way he must regard every person as a responsibility. As the Apostle Paul expressed it, "I am a debtor." In the Old Testament the question is asked, "Am I my brother's keeper?" The Christian answer is, "I am my brother's brother." When a person looks upon the other person as a brother, he senses immediately what his responsibility is. There cannot be any artificial classifying of brothers. Every person is my responsibility, and as a Christian I dare not evade it!

While it is true that some people are much more easily approached than others, the fact remains that one soul is just as dear and precious to God as another, and who are we to draw a line and say that this person shall have the gospel and this person shall not? This does not mean that it is not proper to have a church in one place and not in another, or to conduct a missions program in one place and not in another. Because we are not able to go into all the world at one and the same time we must reach people where we can. But we must not become content with those we have reached. So long as there remains one lost soul on the face of the earth, Christians have a responsibility to that soul. He is a responsibility. Henry Drummond once said: "Every atom in the universe can act on every other atom, but only through the atom next to it. And if a man would act upon every other man he can do it best by acting, one at a time, upon those beside him."

Know the People You Try to Win

Look at every person against his own background. There are a number of contributing factors that go into the making up of every life. Heredity and environment play a big part here, as does individual choice. While it is true that the whole human race is born in sin—that is, with a depraved tendency toward sin—it is also true that some are more sinful than others. God declares in the Old Testament: "I the Lord thy God am a jealous God, visiting the iniquity of the fathers upon the children unto the third and fourth generation of them that hate me" (Exod. 20:5). The depravity of some parents, along with the environment in which they rear their children, makes it extremely difficult to bring an effective witness to bear upon their household. The only way the condition can be changed is through the love and devotion of an understanding and wise witness for Christ. In every age, those who have excelled in this work have been possessed with such love for people that they have exposed themselves to strange sights, bad smells, and those who are morally debauched in order to bring men and women to Christ.

The greatest single factor in any person's life is the power of choice. "Choices are," as described by John Oxenham, "the hinges of destiny." It is here that the Christian witness has his greatest opportunity. No life is so degraded by heredity and enslaved by environment that it cannot be redeemed if the choice of the individual can be directed towards Christ. The person who helps direct this choice must be able to see beyond the immediate and glimpse the ultimate possibilities of divine grace. An u n k n o w n preacher visited a gypsy camp outside of London, England, one day. Before he left the camp he saw a tousle-haired, dirty-faced, ragged boy. He called the boy to him, told him the story of Jesus, prayed for the boy to grow up and become a preacher. He did. That boy was none other than Gipsy Smith, who later became the great evangelist.

Respect the Individual Conscience

It is the function of the human conscience to assess moral quality to all the thoughts and actions of an individual. If these are regarded to be right, conscience, approves; if they are not regarded to be right, conscience condemns. Conscience, however, is not a safe guide unless it is properly enlightened. The purpose of the gospel is to furnish conscience with a norm by which all thoughts and actions can be tested.

But there are varying degrees of knowledge and understanding of the gospel. Each person is responsible to the extent of his own knowledge and understanding. As knowledge increases, responsibility increases accordingly. It is at this point that older and more mature Christians sometimes encounter difficulty in helping others get established in Christian experience. They fail to respect the conscience of the individual they are trying to win and frequently demand of him a pattern of conduct that only informed and seasoned Christians live. The idea here is not that there are varying standards of Christian conduct; but to emphasize strongly that personal knowledge of the gospel is the measure of personal accountability. Christian witnesses need to be careful that they do not demand more of a convert than does the gospel.

Emphasize Positive Christian Living

The New Testament is not a series of negations or "Thou shalt not's." To be sure, it does forbid certain practices and excludes those who do not regard its demands from inheriting the kingdom of God. But the main emphasis of the New Testament is positive and demands action. "This do, and thou shalt live" is the advice Christ gave to a lawyer who desired to inherit eternal life. Repentance is more than turning away from sin; this is only halfway repentance. To be complete, repentance requires a rightabout-face, a completely reversed position before God.

What a person gets when he becomes a Christian far

outweighs anything he may have to give up in order to become a Christian. Too long have Christians let the unsaved think of religion as a kill-joy experience. For those who take their religion seriously enough to work at the job of really being Christian, "godliness is profitable unto all things, having promise of the life that now is, and of that which is to come" (I Tim. 4:8). It pays to live right, and Christians would do well to talk more to this point when they witness to others. It pays with a clean conscience, a pure heart, a daily source of strength and inspiration for service, and an eternal hope.

Use the Word of God

Every Christian should know his Bible and how to use it in winning others to Christ. There is absolutely no excuse for ignorance of the Word of God, especially of the New Testament and its message about Christ and the Holy Spirit. The study of the Bible should be a part of the spiritual diet daily. "Read it to be wise, practice it to be holy" is an adage worth remembering and practicing. But how can people practice the Bible if they do not know its teachings? How can people be witnesses of the gospel if they know not the gospel? An indispensable requisite for soul-winning is a working knowledge of the Bible and how to apply its teachings to the needs of men and women today.

The Word of God is not static. "But the word of God grew and multiplied" (Acts 12:24). It grew in transformed lives and informed minds. The Word of God grows with every convert to Christianity; at least such should be true. Christians are described by Paul as "living epistles, known and read of men." This being true, every Christian should be so well versed in the Scriptures and so dedicated to the practice of their precepts that should someone choose to follow this life he would not be led astray.

Make No Compromise with Sin

It is expected that those who seek to win sinners to Christ should themselves live sinless lives. The person with sin in his own life cannot speak convincingly to a sinner about Christ. In order to live sinlessly, it is necessary that one have a good understanding of what is sin. Many err at the point of classifying mistakes which result from a lack of knowledge as sin. But according to the Word of God sin is always a willful and volitional act or omission. There is no such thing as unwillful sin. When a man loves God with all his heart, soul, mind, and strength, imperfect though his knowledge may be, yet he does not sin against God. "Whosoever is born of God doth not commit sin; for his seed remaineth in him: and he cannot sin, because he is born of God" (I John 3:9). God is love; his seed is love, and when God's love is in the heart of man it restrains him from sinning.

In helping others find Christ, do not encourage a profession of religion so long as there remains sin in the seeker's life. Sound instruction is needed here. The steps to salvation need to be clearly outlined to the penitent soul. A compromise here can be fatal, for if he is led into a profession of religion without really experiencing Christ he will be in a worse spiritual condition than before. Jesus said concerning the kingdom of God that "the violent take it by force" (Matt. 11:12). Men have to force sin out of their lives by a complete surrender of their wills to Christ. This does not make salvation the work of man, something man does for himself, but it does point out the absolute necessity of man's exercising his will in helping extract sin from his own heart and life. Christ can save no man until he is willing to be saved, and no man is ready to be saved unless he is willing to relinquish the hold of sin upon his life.

Establish Points of Agreement; Don't Argue

The Christian is a witness of the claims of Christ and the power of his gospel. Christ's claims need no defense and his gospel needs no vindication. All that is needed is a herald, a witness. "Infallible proofs" have already been set forth by Christ himself. God has already made "this same Jesus . . . both Lord and Christ." Nothing more need be done or can be done to validate the gospel. All that is required of the Christian is to bear witness to what God has done—in history and in his own personal experience.

It is inevitable that some will bring up arguments against becoming a Christian. Christ told at least one parable about people who were always saying, "Excuse me, please." The personal worker today will have to deal with this problem. In doing so, he must not willingly and knowingly give or take offense. There are some people who are just not ready to repent at the time the witness is given, and to insist unduly at such a time will do more harm than good. The best thing to do is to commit such a person to the Lord in prayer and seek to find a more opportune time to lead him to Christ. Luke refers to Lydia in the Book of Acts as a woman "whose heart the Lord opened." The suggestion here is simply that the Christian witness must have the mind of the Lord in any given situation and follow it accordingly. Unless God opens the heart when the witness is given, regardless of how skillful the presentation of the gospel witness, there is no conversion. All the arguments in the world cannot make it otherwise.

Be Alert to Witnessing Opportunities

Someone has observed: "Opportunity does not come to the person who waits for it, but to the person who makes it." In the matter of helping others find Christ, this is largely true. Occasionally someone may come and ask for help, but usually the Christian must assume the initiative and proceed by use of his best judgment and the guidance of the Holy Spirit. All about us are people without Christ. We pass them on the street, ride with them on the bus, live with them in a community, and talk with them about most everything else. But too often when it comes to religion we remain silent and they remain lost. If our neighbors and friends and fellow citizens are ever won to Christ, we have got to muster up enough courage and pray for enough grace to go where they are and invite them to Christ. Every person presents a witnessing opportunity if we can only find the avenue of approach. Here we need the help of the Lord.

The thing that makes the Acts of the Apostles such interesting reading is the way the Holy Spirit directed the early Christians in giving their personal witness. There was no reluctance on their part to speak; indeed, the problem was to keep them silent! When forbidden to speak about Christ, they answered: "We cannot but speak the things we have seen and heard." The Holy Spirit within them made their opportunities for them and directed them where and how and to whom to give their witness. Every Christian was a witness and spoke with the certainty born of a living experience with Christ. Their motivation came from within, a fire burned in their hearts, and it would not be quenched. "Be filled with the Spirit" is the simple recipe for those who would be soul winners.

If You Fail, Try Again

Too many times witnesses for Christ fail in their efforts because their primary purpose is to get results. Results are good and desirable, and certainly they are to be welcomed when they come. But when they are not forthcoming, there is no need for discouragement. Getting the witness to people is the task. Duty is ours; results belong to God.

One of the severest tests to which the witness for Christ is subjected comes when he has put forth his best effort to win someone to Christ and fails. Does he have grace of soul and strength of character to try again? When such an experience comes, it is well to remember that our Lord "witnessed a good confession before Pontius Pilate" and failed in his efforts. Did he cease trying? Paul reasoned with Felix of "righteousness, temperance, and judgment to come" and failed in his efforts to convert him. Did he quit trying? There is no stopping place for the Christian witness. "He that putteth his hand to the plow and looketh back is not fit for the kingdom of God," are the words of Jesus Christ.

PARISH EVANGELISM

Already we have noted that the Christian religion cannot live separate and apart from the local church. At the heart of Christianity is what we call fellowship. Those who are Christian naturally gravitate together for the purpose of worship and corporate effort in bringing others to Christ. The local church is indispensable in the work of evangelism. It is the center from which the individual Christian works to make disciples. God has ordained that it be so. Therefore it is expedient that in our study of helping others find Christ we give some thought to practical methods whereby members of a local congregation can work together in making a corporate impact upon the hearts of men.

The Pastor Enlists, Trains, Directs

God, in his infinite wisdom, has so organized the local church that he has ordained some to be "pastors and teachers; for the perfecting of the saints, for the work of the ministry, for the edifying of the body of Christ: till we all come in the unity of the faith, and of the knowledge of the Son of God, unto a perfect man, unto the measure of the stature of the fullness of Christ" (Eph. 4:11-13). This divinely inspired word by the Apostle Paul clearly marks out the work of the pastor and suggests his importance in the local congregation.

The pastor is the keyman in the program of evangelism in the local parish. Upon him, more than upon any other person, falls the responsibility of giving direction to the evangelistic outreach of the church he serves. He is called of God and by the people for this purpose, and he dare not neglect his responsibility. In the normal situation, no other member of the congregation wields wider influence or speaks with greater moral authority. If the church and the gospel are to be perpetuated the pastor must do his work thoroughly and efficiently.

Yet no pastor can succeed in his work without the help of God and the co-operation of the people he serves. Every Christian in his rightful place and serving to the extent of his ability is the divine pattern. In the local congregation, and there in a more real way than anywhere else, Christians are "workers together with God." There are some things which can be done only when Christians work together. In the New Testament we read of four men who worked together in bringing another man to Christ. One man, two men,

even three men, could not have done the job. The
principle here is capable of broad application. The
greater the task to which a local church commits itself,
the greater the need for co-operation in achieving
success. The pastor's work is largely that of enlisting,
training, and directing others for these co-operative
tasks.

Successful pastors have found it expedient to devote considerable time to training others to do the
work of evangelism. This has been done by conducting
special training classes, the pairing and directing of
visitation teams, and by preaching sermons that set
forth the principles of soul-winning. Some pastors
have found it helpful to appoint a committee to help
in co-ordinating the program of evangelism in the local
church. This committee helps in the development of
responsibility lists, the planning of visitation and revival campaigns, and in keeping alive the evangelistic
emphasis in every department and organization of
the church. Each pastor and congregation will have
to develop the kind of organization and program that
best fits the local needs and resources.

Church School Wins Most

During the past three centuries the church school
has helped millions find and live for Christ. Bringing
all age groups together on the Lord's Day for a period
of Bible study and character education has proved
effective and practical. A survey in almost any church
would demonstrate that the majority of the members
have been won through the teaching ministry of the
church school. Teachers, therefore, should not mini-
mize the importance of their efforts but should recognize that to them has been committed one of the
greatest ministries of the church. The work may appear
to be slow and gradual, and it is, but the finished

product in Christian character is compensation supreme.

It has been demonstrated time and time again that one of the best ways to reach adults is to take an active interest in their children. The prophetic utterance concerning Christ—"A little child shall lead them"— emphasizes a principle of leadership that the church cannot afford to overlook. While it is not possible to rear and educate a child in such a way that the new birth will not be necessary, it is possible to surround a child with influences that will incline his heart toward God.

It is here that the church must direct its most skillful and most potent witness. What any child becomes will depend largely upon the efforts put forth to direct his life. The wrong word, the wrong action, and a child's life can be blighted for time and eternity. "Do not sin against the child" is a scriptural exhortation that should be heeded by every parent and every teacher of religion. Not every experience that a child has with God is a conversion experience, and a serious injustice is done against a child when he is urged to seek Christ before he knows what he is doing.

Some pastors, in order to eliminate undue risks in the spiritual development of the children, have organized pastor's classes for the purpose of teaching the rudiments of Christian living. In bringing children to conversion, parents, teachers, pastor, or whoever takes the initiative, should not motivate the child by fear but by love. Fear, especially in the heart of a child, can easily become exaggerated beyond its useful purpose in building a right concept of God.

Some few years ago, Irene Smith Caldwell wrote a book entitled: *Our Concern Is Children.* That title suggests a motto for every local congregation. Any church that will make children its concern will be a growing church.

But the church school is not for children only. An invitation to church and Sunday school should never be substituted for an invitation to Christ, but getting a new person to attend church school is frequently the first step in leading that person to Christ. It has happened a thousand times over. The essential thing is to keep the church-school program alive with evangelistic interest.

Men Best Witnesses to Men

What would a church be like without men in it? I know! I was once pastor of such a church! But it is an abnormal situation, for the church belongs to everybody who by repentance and faith will qualify for membership in it. Certainly the church needs men —men of vision, courage, faith, and compelling love. Christ needs men in making his witness known to others. There is a distinct work which only men can do. Some men, for one reason or another, have not faced up to their Christian responsibility as they ought. The purpose here is to amplify some practical ways whereby men can render effective service for God.

In recent years there have developed a number of excellent ideas for intensifying the witness of men for Christ. One such idea is expressed through organizing what is called the Fisherman's Club. The idea for such a club or fellowship is drawn from the call of Christ: "Follow me, and I will make you to become fishers of men." The purpose of the club is simply that of winning men for Christ by a man-to-man witness. A small, lapel-size fishhook has been designed to indicate membership in the club. The insignia helps to open opportunities for witnessing—

there seems to be a somewhat natural tie between men and fish!

Elton Trueblood has interested many in an Order of the Yoke which is a fellowship of those concerned in winning men to Christ. The members wear an ox yoke in their lapels. As people note the yoke and ask about it there is an opportunity for talking with them about Christ and what he can do for them.

Another idea taking hold in some churches is the St. Andrew's Fellowship Club, which seeks to build a closer tie of fellowship between men and boys. The idea is drawn from Andrew's statement to Jesus: "There is a lad here." The purpose of the club is to make every man in the church responsible for at least one boy, not his own son. It is the assignment of every man to see to it that the boy assigned to him is in church every Sunday. Once each quarter, or at a time determined by the fellowship, a supper is given to bring the men and boys together in a group for fellowship, fun, and worship. The idea encourages regularity in church attendance and builds a fellowship between men and boys that extends across the years.

Women Influence Many to Christ

If men are important in the work of evangelism, women are equally so. Christ has made use of dedicated Christian women since the beginning of the church. In his work, there is no distinction of office or order between men and women. Though some would exclude women from any place of responsible leadership in the church, basing their objections on Paul's statement, "Let your women keep silence in the church," a more careful study of Paul's writings reveals that he placed women on a plane equal with men and recognized them as leaders of equal standing with men in the church.

Our purpose here, however, is not to defend women's rights in the church, but to discuss some practical ways whereby women are rendering evangelistic and missionary service to the church. Regardless of what some may think about whether they should or not, the simple fact is that women are preaching and witnessing, and God is blessing their efforts.

In the Church of God we have an organization for women known as the Woman's Missionary Society. This is a national organization with local organizations within a goodly number of the local congregations around the world. Though the organization is comparatively young, it has justified its existence. At the present time this organization is doing an aggressive work of educating people in the cause of missions, both at home and abroad. The primary purpose of the Society is not to raise money, but to broaden knowledge, understanding, and concern for peoples around the world. When the program of the Society* is followed, it brings into the local church an evangelistic and missionary incentive and challenge that are compelling and motivating.

In the average church it is easier to get women than men to volunteer to do visitation evangelism, and they do effective work. Women also do excellent work as teachers in the church school, counselors for the youth group, and as general church workers. In the shop, in the office, on the street, and in the home women can and should use their influence for the Master.

Youth Make Effective Witnesses

Among young people are to be found some of the Lord's most effective witnesses. For the most part, young people take their religion seriously. The twen-

---

*For information concerning the local organization of the Society write: National Woman's Missionary Society, Box 68, Anderson, Ind.

tieth century with its two world wars and danger of a
third has not been kind to young people. Yet an excit-
ing and thrilling surge of spiritual power has been
moving in the hearts of our youth. The great majority
of those accepting Christ in these days are from among
the ranks of our young people. This is as it should be,
but it has not always been so. If this potential for
evangelism can be properly directed, this century will
write a new chapter in Christian missions and evangelism.

Young people can win other young people. Among
no other group in society is the herd instinct more
pronounced. Young people, for the most part, do things
together. And into whatever they do they put their
whole hearts. What they need is understanding and
an opportunity to identify themselves with a cause
greater than themselves. In the schoolroom, on the
bus, at the ball game, or wherever young people con-
gregate the Christian witness is needed. One young
person testified recently: "I saw God for the first time
on a basketball floor." To most people that would be
a strange place to see God, but not to a young person.
What this young person meant was that a boy on the
team was a real Christian and that he revealed God
to others.

Organize for Visitation Evangelism

With some modifications, there has been a recovery
in recent years of "two-by-two" visitation evangelism
as initiated by Christ during his ministry. Though the
plan has been abused greatly by some church groups
more concerned about getting church members than
about making disciples for Christ, the method has
merit and when used properly is very effective in
reaching new people for Christ. There is this distinct
advantage to the plan—it reaches people *where they*

live instead of waiting for them to come to church to hear the gospel. The plan calls for a person-to-person conversation about Christ. For the successful use of the plan the following steps are recommended:

Develop a responsibility list. This can be done by the pastor or by some committee appointed by the pastor or church. The responsibility list can be compiled from the following sources: A religious census or survey; unchurched parents of Sunday-school children; unreached members of church families; friendship contacts of church members; visitors at the worship services and other meetings of the church; relatives of church members; attendants at funerals, weddings, and other community contacts of the pastor; newcomers into the community reported through Chamber of Commerce or Welcome Wagon organizations.

Enlist and train visitors. After the responsibility list has been compiled, determine how many visitors will be required to contact the persons on the list within a reasonable length of time. Select the needed number of visitors carefully from among the membership of the local congregation. This job can best be done by the pastor or by some committee selected by the pastor. It has been found wise to hand-pick the persons to do this type of work. Ideally, every Christian is a witness; practically, not all are gifted in the art of entering someone else's home and talking with him about Christ. The selection of visitors can best be obtained by personal interview by the pastor, and the selection should be made several weeks before the actual campaign to allow for proper training. Visitors should include both men and women, the strongest and most capable Christians in the church. Those who have used the plan successfully have found that it takes about ten teams of two each to visit one hundred homes in a period of four nights, which is the usual length of time for such a campaign.

In training the visitors, it is well to have at least four full evenings of training before the actual week of visitation and then a brief training session each evening during that week. Some churches like to have a supper in connection with the training session during the week of visitation, but the campaign can be conducted without it. There is an advantage, however, in having the visitors together at the church for final instruction and prayer before they go forth.

From the Mid-Century Evangelistic Advance of the Church of God, Box 548, Anderson, Indiana, you can obtain materials for training visitors, a turn-over chart entitled *They Went Forth Two by Two* with supplementary help for the pastor; also a filmstrip on how to make the contact in the home and other helps. Ask for a listing of their materials.

The assignment of prospects to the visiting teams should be made with the greatest possible care. The pairing of teams is also of great importance. Husband and wife should always be paired together unless some unusual situation should necessitate men and women visiting separately. The same team should work together throughout the campaign, with the teammates alternating in leading the interviews in the home. As much information as possible should be given each team regarding the persons to be visited. This information should be on a card containing the prospect's name and address so that it can be reread before entering the home.

"Into whatever house ye enter" try for decision. The time comes to enter the house of the person whose name is on the responsibility list. Here is where the test really comes. Everything done before is only preparatory. Success now will depend upon how much

has been learned through the periods of training, plus
the ability of the visitors to apply what they have
learned. How shall the house be entered?

Charles Lamb once said: "There are few things that
fill the heart with such great expectation as a knock
on the door." When the door opens, what then? The
first thing is for the visitors to give their names and
clearly state the purpose of their call in the home.
When the invitation is given to enter, visitors should
seek ways of creating a friendly atmosphere. But immediately the conversation must be turned to the primary purpose of the visit, or time will pass and the
opportunity be lost. Each team of visitors will have
to gauge just how far to go in the initial visit in
bringing the conversation to a point of decision. It
cannot be stressed too strongly that the object here
is that of securing definite decisions and conversions
to Christ. Sometimes this cannot be done in one interview, but whether the interviews be one or many,
this is the objective to keep clearly in mind. Regardless of the outcome of the visit, the visitor should keep
a record of the response and give it to the pastor.

Follow up the gains you make. It is not likely that
all of the persons whose names are on the responsibility list will be at home when the call is made. Visitors should note the absentees and call again. When
persons not won by the first visit show interest in becoming Christians, the visitors should plan to return
at a later date and cultivate the opportunity of bringing those persons to Christ. All definite decisions
should be reported immediately to the pastor so he can
call in the home, strengthen the decision, and help
the newly won converts to take their places in the
church.

Continue program of evangelism. There is no need
for this method of evangelism to be discontinued after

a special campaign. It is capable of perpetual use in the church. One congregation sends out visitors every Wednesday night while the rest of the church engage in prayer for their success. By keeping the responsibility list alive and the visitors active, the program can go on endlessly. Certainly it will bear repeating several times during the year. Some churches find it profitable to conduct a visitation campaign in conjunction with a special preaching mission or revival meeting. The important thing is to keep the evangelistic spirit alive among the members of the congregation.

Use Mass Evangelism Carefully

History records that the church of God began in a prayer meeting which was followed by preaching and the saving of many souls. Ever since, the church has made use of mass assemblies in bringing others to Christ. Sometimes this method has fallen into disrepute because of some who have catered strongly to sensationalism and self-exaltation, yet the method continues to be most useful. In fact, the primary purpose of preaching is that of making a mass appeal for Christ. Our Lord often spoke to crowds of people and won many followers, and his disciples have used it effectively since. A careful study of how to conduct a revival campaign or mass meeting will eliminate, or reduce to a minimum, the questionable aspects of the method.

The earnestness and directness of revival preaching, together with the fact that so many are thinking and talking about Christ at the same time, tend to create an atmosphere in which people are easily led to Christ. The aroused interest and personal efforts of individual Christians help to make meetings of this kind a success. Usually, revival services are better planned for the creation of expectancy and decision on the part of the unsaved than are the regular services of the church, but such need not be so. Regular services can be evangelistic and appealing, too.

Perhaps the most serious fault with mass evangelism is the undue emphasis placed upon numbers. The evangelist who reports the greatest number of "converts" generally gets the most calls. Sometimes the striving for numbers leads to the use of mob psychology, and individuals are induced to engage in some mass movement of the congregation without proper reason. However, a group response may constitute for some a first step toward salvation, when it is properly motivated and controlled. The error lies in accepting such response as an end in evangelism without bringing seekers into conscious fellowship with Christ. In the handling of a crowd, there is always danger that the individual will be overlooked, and when the emotional fervor that prompted his movement with the group dies down, he is liable to slip back into his former state of separation from God.

One of the most effective ways to benefit from mass meetings is to train a sufficient number of altar workers to give individual guidance to seekers. Improper altar work will not produce good converts. One altar worker with each seeker has been found effective in keeping the mind of the seeker from being distracted from the real purpose of his coming forward. The altar worker needs an understanding of human personality; he also needs to know how to instruct others in finding Christ. A record of the names and addresses of persons converted in a mass meeting should be kept for the pastor.

SUGGESTIONS FOR THE CLASS

Method is indispensable to work. It cannot be substituted for work, yet work cannot be done without it. This lesson has set forth certain practical methods that individuals and churches have used in helping others find Christ.

1. Memorize the Great Commission of Christ as recorded by Matthew and Mark. How can this commission best be carried out?

2. What personal qualifications must one possess before he can successfully help others find Christ?

3. Describe the methods and techniques of the most efficient soul winner you know.

4. Why is the local congregation of such great importance to the individual Christian?

5. What organized plan of evangelism do members of your congregation follow in bringing others to Christ? Is it working? If not, why not? Is it a fault of the method or of the persons using the method?

6. Visit a growing congregation and note the plan followed in winning others.

7. How can a revival or mass meeting best be planned?

How was Church of God Reformation started?

CHAPTER V

MORE WAYS OF WINNING OTHERS

The ways of winning others to Christ are as varied as the personalities and abilities of individual Christians. Thus far we have studied how the Christian can help others personally and in co-operation with other Christians in the local congregation. But the Christian's responsibility does not end here. The church was born with a map of the world in its hands, and every Christian has a commission to "go into all the world, and preach the gospel to every creature." In and through and beyond the local church the Christian must make his witness to the world. How can this be done?

PROJECT EVANGELISM

Project evangelism as used in this chapter means specifically that sort of evangelism which can be accomplished only through agencies or institutions set up for the purpose. It is not physically possible for a person to be at more than one place at a time, but he can be in many places by projection of thought, prayer, or gift. Therefore Christians have found it expedient to create such organizations as are needful in making the gospel known to others, and then giving of their moral and financial support to these organizations or agencies.

We Evangelize Through World Service

Over the years the ministers of the Church of God have set up various organizations for the specific purpose of meeting varying needs in the church's educational, evangelistic, or missionary program. Today those agencies are represented by the World Service Commission of the Church of God. Each year the ministers of the church approve and adopt a budget for the operation of the World Service agencies. Individuals and congregations give their support to the World Service Commission, and the money is prorated among the various boards and agencies. Or money may be sent directly to any agency of the church in which the individual has a special interest. Christians should feel a moral responsibility for the financial support of the causes represented by the national agencies of the church.

We Evangelize Through State Agencies

Not only have national organizations been set up for the meeting of world needs. Across the nation and also in Canada, state and provincial organizations have been created for the specific purpose of starting and developing new churches in unreached areas and of strengthening weak churches. Support for this work comes from the churches within the state or province. Many new churches have been started in the past few years. Certainly this method of evangelism is scriptural and deserving of support. "I robbed other churches, taking wages of them, to do you service" (II Cor. 11:8), says Paul. His statement infers that other churches supported him as he worked to develop the church in Corinth.

How Project Evangelistic Effort?

There are a number of ways in which a Christian can help others find Christ through project evangelism. The list here contains only a few:

Support a foreign missionary. Information concerning how this can be done will be furnished by the

Missionary Board of the Church of God, Anderson, Indiana, upon request. Many opportunities are presently open to the Church of God in countries where we do not currently have mission stations. The church is constantly expanding its missionary frontiers as trained personnel and available funds permit.

Pay a student's way through college. No better investment can be made than in the training of Christian young people for service to the Christian cause. Many young people, who have been divinely called of God, will never have the opportunity of a college education unless someone helps make it possible. Anderson College and Theological Seminary, Anderson, Indiana; Pacific Bible College, Portland, Oregon; and Alberta Bible Institute, Camrose, Alberta, Canada, will furnish information about worthy students upon request.

Build a church in a new place. America today is a nation on wheels and wings. People are migrating from one place to another at an astounding rate of speed. Many of these people were good Christians back in the home community, but now they are uprooted spiritually. They need the church, but many of them are located in a town or city where there is no congregation of the Church of God. With a little help these people can get a new church started. The Board of Church Extension and Home Missions is constantly in contact with these new opportunities and will gladly furnish information.

Sponsor the Christian Brotherhood Hour radio broadcast. For the past several years the Church of God has conducted an international radio program known as the Christian Brotherhood Hour. The broadcast has reached untold millions with the gospel witness and has opened many opportunities before the Church of God. By paying for the thirty-minute radio time over your local station you can help bring this witness to your neighbors and friends. The program urges "A United Church for a Divided World," which is the great need in the world today. Upon request the Radio Commission of the Church of God will give information regarding the cost of airing the program. Address Box 2000, Anderson, Indiana.

Distribute gospel literature. The Church of God maintains its own publishing house and each year prints and distributes millions of pieces of gospel literature. Tons of free literature are sent out to different parts of the world annually. It is free only to the receiver; somebody has to pay for it, for no one can print literature without cost. By the distribution of tracts, books, and Bibles you can help others find Christ. The Free Literature Department, Gospel Trumpet Company, Anderson, Indiana, will accept your contribution and will send literature wherever you direct.

Make available a home missionary. The population of America includes a number of minority groups, some of whom are greatly underprivileged and needy of the gospel. The American Indians, the Spanish-speaking people of the Southwest, the Negroes, the mountain people of Kentucky and other states, and many other minority groups are our responsibility and need our help. The Division of Home Missions, Board of Church Extension and Home Missions, Anderson, Indiana, will give information about home missions work.

Help set up a church building loan fund. One of the greatest needs in the church today is a revolving loan fund from which low-interest loans can be made to developing churches. Such a fund would be perpetual in its use. It is not easy for new churches to obtain loans, as they have no local reputation or financial security. A revolving loan fund would be of invaluable help in getting more churches started. The Division of Evangelism, Board of Church Extension and Home Missions, Anderson, Indiana, is developing such a fund and will gladly furnish information concerning how to contribute to it.

The ways suggested here are ways others have found to evangelize. There are many, many more.

THESE FOUND WAYS TO WIN THEIR FELLOWS

Andrew Brought Peter

When Andrew found Christ for himself he went immediately to tell his brother, "We have found the Christ." Thus was begun his soul-winning career. Almost every time this man's name is mentioned he is helping someone come to Jesus. He it was, at the time when the multitude followed Jesus into the desert place, who discovered the lad with the loaves and fishes. When certain Greeks came to see and hear Jesus, it was Andrew who told the Master of their presence. Quiet, reserved, overshadowed by his brother, yet he found a way—and took it.

Philip Won Many

The story of Philip is one of the most illuminating in the New Testament. He first comes into the history of the early church when it was having trouble. A controversy over the distribution of food arose among certain members of the Jerusalem church. The apostles, in order to devote themselves to prayer and to the ministry of the Word, suggested that a committee of seven men be selected to handle the ministration of food. Philip was one of the men selected to serve on the committee, but not for long. God had his hand on this man for greater work.

We read of Philip next in the city of Samaria, "preaching the things concerning the kingdom of God, and the name of Jesus." God blessed his efforts and there "was great joy in that city." But Philip was not to stay long. God wanted him to talk to a lone man, making his way across the desert toward Gaza. This man had been to Jerusalem, but had not found the Lord there, and he was on his way home to Ethiopia. He sat in his chariot reading from the fifty-third chapter of Isaiah. The Spirit directed Philip: "Go near, and join thyself to this chariot." Philip did and led the man to Christ, through the reading of God's Word and giving its true interpretation. He baptized the man, and then God caught him away to another task.

Paul Found a Way

No person in New Testament history had a more cataclysmic conversion than Saul of Tarsus. He was a persecutor and waster of the church. But he was sincere, and so God gave him "a heavenly vision." During the short span of a little more than two decades this man established churches throughout Asia Minor and in parts of Europe.

Perhaps one of the most tender stories about Paul, revealing the true character of the man, is the one in which he pleads with Philemon by letter to forgive his runaway slave, Onesimus, and regard him as a brother in Christ. "I beseech thee for my son Onesimus, whom I have begotten in my bonds: which in time past was to thee unprofitable, but now profitable to thee and to me: whom I have sent again: thou therefore receive him, that is, mine own bowels. . . . If thou count me a partner, receive him as myself. If he hath wronged thee, or oweth thee ought, put that on mine account" (vss. 10-18). "Charge that to my account!" It is no wonder that Paul won souls and built churches for Christ. He found a way! "Charge that to my account!"

A Church Met in Their House

Paul met Priscilla and Aquila for the first time in Corinth. They had fled there when "Claudius had commanded all Jews to depart from Rome." When Paul was preaching in Corinth Priscilla and Aquila opened their home to him, and since they, too, were tentmakers they shared their work with Paul. Later Priscilla and Aquila went to Ephesus. There they heard Apollos preach in one of the synagogues. He was an "eloquent man, and mighty in the scriptures." But he knew only the baptism of John. Priscilla and Aquila took "him unto them, and expounded unto him the way of God more perfectly." This man became a great witness for Christ. "He mightily convinced the Jews, and that publicly, showing by the scriptures that Jesus was Christ" (Acts 18:28). Priscilla and Aquila made their way back to Rome. Paul wrote the Christians there, "Greet Priscilla and Aquila, my helpers in Christ Jesus: who have for my life laid down their own necks. . . . Likewise greet the church that is in their house" (Rom. 16:3-5).

Francis of Assisi Trained Others

John Bernadone was born at Assisi, Italy, in 1182. His father was a prosperous cloth merchant and through his journeys to France was enabled to initiate his son into the language and customs of the French. It was on account of his fondness for the French people that John received the name "Francis." During his early life he indulged in the dissipations common to the wealthy youth of that period, but severe illness brought him face to face with the solemn questions of life. He experienced a restlessness of soul that was satisfied only when he met Jesus Christ and accepted him as Lord and Savior. Then he renounced all of his wealth and identified himself with the poor. In his own words, he set out "naked, to follow the naked Christ."

Gradually he collected a band of followers who went about the lanes and towns of Tuscany, helping in the harvest or doing any casual work, sleeping in the open or wherever they could, tending the outcasts and lepers. The story of his life and the order he developed spread to other lands. By his death in 1226 there had spread across Europe a band of devoted men who reveled in poverty, smiled at hardship, bore with patience and joy the persecutions that came. Francis found a way.

Luther Against a World

On an April evening over four hundred years ago a simple monk stood before the emperor of the Holy Roman Empire and spoke words that have echoed through the centuries: "My conscience is captive to the Word of God. I cannot and I will not recant anything, for to go against my conscience is neither right nor safe. Here I stand." And he did stand, as one man against the world. And because he stood the structure of medieval Catholicism was shattered and a new day dawned for the cause of Christ. The day Luther took his stand for Christ and conscience marked a new day in the advancement of Christianity. What if he had not taken his stand? He found a way—and took it!

John Wesley Gave Them Christ

Back of every man is a woman—his mother. The mother of John Wesley was an exceptional woman. The mother of nineteen children, John being the fifteenth, Susannah Wesley was a woman of unusual wisdom and organizational ability. On the fifth birthday of each child, she taught him or her the alphabet;

the next day she taught the child to read the first sentence in the Bible. When John was only six years of age, the Wesley home burned, and John was rescued at the last minute. His mother made a covenant with God following this experience, as follows: "I do intend to be more particularly careful with the soul of this child . . . than ever I had been, that I may instill into his mind the principles of true religion and virtue." The whole world now knows about the fulfillment of that dedication.

When John Wesley entered the ministry, his mother counseled, "The true end of preaching is to mend men's lives and not to stuff their heads with unprofitable speculation." For several years, John did not really know the Lord, but an experience one night in Aldersgate Street in London changed the course of his life— and of the world. John began to preach to mend men's lives. It is said that in fifty years he traveled, mostly on horseback, more than 225,000 miles and preached forty thousand sermons, averaging eight hundred sermons a year. At the age of eighty-five, over a period of eight weeks, he preached eighty times. He preached everywhere and under all kinds of conditions. One night after he had preached, he retired to his room and wrote in his diary: "I gave them Christ!"

Thank God for a man like Wesley. He found a way!

Asbury Won the American Frontier

There stands in Washington, D.C., a statue of a man astride a horse. On the base of the statue are inscribed these words: "If you would see the results of his labors, you will find them in our Christian civilization." That statue is of a man named Francis Asbury, who on September 4, 1771, at the age of twenty-six and at the call of John Wesley for missionaries to go to America, boarded a ship in Bristol, England, for the

long voyage to America. Midsea on the trip, Asbury
made this entry in his diary: "Whither am I going? To
the new world. What to do? To gain honor? Not if I
know my heart. To get money? No! I am going to live
to God, and to bring others so to do."

Upon reaching America, he labored for thirty years
for thirty dollars a year. His *Journal* indicates that he
preached over sixteen thousand sermons and in forty-
five years traveled more miles than did John Wesley,
crossing the Allegheny Mountains more than sixty
times. Everywhere Asbury went souls were led to
Christ. His was largely a ministry to the people settling
the frontier. He found a way "to live in God, and
bring others to do so."

Warner Led a Reformation

On December 13, 1877, Daniel Sidney Warner wrote
a covenant in which he utterly dedicated his life to
the Lord Jesus Christ. First he set forth God's promise
as recorded in Jeremiah 31:33 and then added his own
acceptance of God's covenant. A condensation of the
covenant* he wrote reads as follows:

Lord, thou hast been true to thy covenant, though I have
been most unfaithful and am now altogether unworthy to
take hold of thy most gracious covenant. But knowing
that thou hast bound thyself in thy free offer to "be merci-
ful to their unrighteousness," I take courage to approach
thee and would most earnestly beseech thee to fulfill thy
wonderful offer to BE MY GOD; and I do most joyfully
yield myself entirely TO BE THINE.

Therefore this soul which thou hast made in thine
own image is placed wholly in thy hands to do with it as
seemeth good.

This mind shall think only for thy glory and the pro-
motion of thy cause.

This will is thy will, O God!

Birth of a Reformation, by A. L. Byers. Out of print, but in many
church libraries.

The spirit within this body is now thine; do with it as thou wilt, in life, and in death.

This body is thy temple forever.

These hands shall work only for thee.

These eyes to see thy adorable works and thy holy law.

This tongue and these lips to speak only holiness unto the Lord.

These ears to hear thy voice alone.

These feet to walk only in thy ways.

And all my being is now and forever thine.

.   .   .   .

In covenant with the God of all grace and mercy, who has become my salvation, my all, and whose I am forever, to the praise of his glory.

Entered into by the direction of the Holy Spirit and signed this thirteenth day of December, in the year of our Lord eighteen hundred and seventy-seven.

—DANIEL SIDNEY WARNER

For the following eighteen years, till his death on December 12, 1895, Daniel Sidney Warner lived a rich and full life in the ministry, preaching in most of the states across the nation, writing songs and sermons, printing and distributing the *Gospel Trumpet*, planting truth and building churches, experiencing persecutions and facing the hardships of frontier life. Yet his covenant with God held true. Moved with the conviction that God's church was one and that all Christians should forsake denominations and creeds designed by men and find unity and fellowship in the body of Christ, he kept moving out and beyond with the message of the gospel. It was not unusual for him to preach two or more sermons a day, ranging in length up to four hours, and then spend all or part of the night in writing songs and sermons for distribution. As a result of his labors, along with those of his co-workers, an effective movement towards Christian unity has entered the stream of world Christianity. Time alone will reveal the good accomplished by this humble man of God who found it in his heart to dedicate his life to the Lord. Warner found a way to make his witness effective!

Riggle Won Men with Kindness

The name of H. M. Riggle will long be remembered by Church of God people around the world. He was a great soul, a great preacher, and an effective soul winner. In the making of a great life often the little and unexpected things count most. Two incidents from out of his soul-winning ministry are recorded in *Pioneer Evangelism*.

In one of our revivals a near neighbor was converted. His wife became enraged and very bitter towards us as a result. She said that we had spoiled all her pleasure. Her husband would not take her to the show, theater, or other worldly places of entertainment. Instead, he took interest in church work. When we would pass in front of her house, she would refuse to speak, but would look daggers at us. I said to my wife, "We must win that woman to Christ." We made a large bouquet of flowers and sent them to her home with one of our little girls, who was instructed to tell her, "Here is a little token of love from Papa and Mama to you." The next time we passed her house she came out and greeted us with a smile, and was very friendly ever after. In the very next meeting she came out and got saved.

In the same town lived a wicked man who hated and cursed the brethren. He refused to speak to me when I met him on the street. We decided to win him also. We began by sending gifts through the children. Finally he became friendly. Before we left the place he died; but before he passed away he sent for my wife and me to pray for him that he might be saved. It pays to "live peaceably with all men."

Flowers and gifts, and two souls are led to Christ. Is it any wonder that this man preached great sermons and led hundreds to Christ? He found a way to get beyond the hardness of men's hearts.

Which Way Will You Take?

Christians today are finding a way. Why should I say more? Seeing that "we are compassed about with so great a cloud of witnesses," let us lay aside "every weight" and find a way to help others find Christ. All about us are dedicated Christians who are working diligently at the job, doing their best in whatever ways they can. The task is too great for so few. "The harvest truly is great, but the laborers are few." The question is, Which way will you take?

"Once to every man and nation comes the moment to decide." The present hour demands a choice, what shall it be?

SUGGESTIONS FOR THE CLASS

As John brought his gospel to a close he was aware that there were so many more things he could have written about Jesus that he summed it up: "And there are also many other things which Jesus did, the which, if they should be written every one, I suppose that even the world itself could not contain the books that should be written." Somewhat the same thing could be said regarding the ways by which help can be extended to others. So in this chapter we have tried to close by focusing attention on the world mission of the church and how Christians in every age have found a way to do work for God and help others find Christ.

1. Mark on a map of the world the different places where the Church of God is helping to meet human needs.

2. What is the measure of the Christian's responsibility in the local church? In the world program of the church?

3. What organization for co-operative evangelism has been developed in your state?

4. How was the Church of God reformation movement started?

5. What are some of the methods now being used by Christians in helping others find Christ? Evaluate these methods.

6. Does your local church support the World Missions program of the Church of God? Do you as an individual?

7. Decide on something you can do to help others find Christ—and do it!

If Christ is within there is a out bursting. If there is no outbursting we are made to wander if Christ is within.